MAY 1940: DESTINATION DUNKIRK

The Mission of a "Little Ship"

MICHAEL E WILLS

Published in 2025 by Michael E Wills

Copyright © Michael E Wills 2025

The right of Michael E Wills to be identified as the author of this work has been asserted in accordance with the Copyright, Designs and Patents Act 1988 Sections 77 and 78.

All rights reserved. No part of this publication may be reproduced, stored in a retrieval system, or transmitted in any form or by any means, electronic, mechanical, photocopying, recording or otherwise, without prior permission of the copyright holder.

This book is a work of fiction. Places mentioned in the book are based on fact, and some characters appearing in the story are based on real figures, all of whom are no longer alive.

ISBN 978-1-7392976-9-5

CONTENTS

Introduction 5
Units Used in This Book 9
Chapter 1: Early May, 1940 St John's Approved School 11
Chapter 2: Tuesday Morning, 28th May 1940 24
Chapter 3: Tuesday Morning, 28th May 1940 37
Chapter 4: Tuesday Evening, May 28th 1940 46
Chapter 5: Wednesday Morning, 29th May 1940 53
Chapter 6: Wednesday 29th May 1940, 18.05 66
Chapter 7: Two Hours Earlier 73
Chapter 8: Wednesday 29th May, 1940 - 9.25 hours 78
Chapter 9: Thursday 30th May, 14.00 hours 91
Chapter 10: Friday 31st May, 03.00 hours 105
Chapter 11: Friday 31st May, 13.00 hours 128
Chapter 12: Saturday 1st June, 16.30 hours 146
Chapter 13: Sunday 2nd June, 21.00 hours Ramsgate 156
Chapter 14: 12th May, 1941 Newport 163
Epilogue 167
Other Books by Michael E Wills 173

INTRODUCTION

The writing of this book was a project that I had considered for many years but have always shied away from. Perhaps I should first explain why I have written it and then explain why I never before felt able to do so.

The story of Dunkirk has been written about and filmed extensively and admirably in the past. The whole event which was named Operation Dynamo, was such a mighty undertaking that it demanded a huge canvas to tell the story. However, I wanted to "humanise" the epic event by relating the tale of one "Little Ship" and the people who sailed her to France and witnessed the horrifying spectacle on Dunkirk beach.

I have been aware of Operation Dynamo ever since I can remember because it was a folk legend in the town, on the Isle of Wight, where I was born and grew up. In May 1940, sixteen local merchant sailors volunteered to man motor barges, which were normally used to supply everything the island needed. They agreed to risk their lives to answer the desperate call to help save an army. As I grew up, I met some of these men and regularly saw their ships in Newport Harbour. The vessels were shallow draft, designed to navigate in such depths as the River Medina offered and, when necessary, to settle between tides in its mud.

The operation happened more than eighty years ago and with the passing of time it became part of history. As such, naturally, it is remembered more for the dates it happened and the statistics relating to men saved, and ships lost, than the personal stories of those involved. I wanted to put that right, at least in one small corner of the whole massive enterprise.

In considering the penning of this book I decided to write it in the genre of historical fiction. I did this because although I knew the crew of the ship I write about, there was an imbalance in that knowledge. I knew the captain very well; I was born in his house, and I spent the first five years of my life living there while my father was in the army. I knew the engineer and saw him regularly because in my early teenage years he was a neighbour. What I did not know until very much later was that he was a remarkable man who served with honour and bravery in the First World War. He also recorded both his time fighting in Gallipoli in 1915 and the action he saw at Dunkirk. In this book, I have drawn heavily on the facts in the latter account.

My problem with writing non-fiction was the fact that though I had met the other two crew members of the ship, I knew nothing of their personal stories or their personalities. Out of respect for their descendants I could not invent these. So, to address this imbalance I concluded that the best route was to fictionalise the story, keeping as close as possible to the facts my research gave me, the narrative written by the engineer, and my knowledge of the sea. As regards the latter, my own sailing experience has taken me on the same route along the south coast, even as far as Dunkirk, and I was well aware of the hazards of the voyage.

It is over seventy years since I set foot on the ship in the story and my memory of it is thus distant. I am indebted to Wayne Pritchett, long time Harbour Master in Newport, for his patience in answering my many questions relating to it.

Writing the story as a novel provided an opportunity to dramatise the account and perhaps to appeal to readers not necessarily in possession of my avid interest in history! This format also gave me the chance to address a myth. I have been asked several times about the veracity of the story of a boy, or young man, who was either a stowaway on one of the island ships that sailed to France, or perhaps he had been aboard for a pleasure day trip at the invitation of a crew member relative, neither knowing where their day would end!

As an historian I am keen that the knowledge of things past should not fade into oblivion. With this book I hope that I can contribute towards keeping alive knowledge of a time when Britain was under a greater existential threat than at any time since 1066.

So, why after many years of prevarication did I decide at last to write this story? The simple answer is that I am now in my eighties, and I want to pass on to others the knowledge I have about the ship, the sailors, and their adventure, before it is too late.

Michael E Wills
October 2025

UNITS USED IN THIS BOOK

When I started research for this novel, I immediately became aware of the fact that telling a story using units of measurements of distance, depth of the sea, weight, and so on, which were in use in 1940, might confuse a modern reader.

However, not using terms familiar to the characters in the book would make dialogue somewhat artificial. I therefore decided to use units of measure familiar over eighty years ago and to explain them to the reader in this preface.

Also included are some units of measurement still in use today, though not internationally. I also thought that some readers unfamiliar with nautical terms might like them defined.

I am aware, too, that we are very much at a crossroads in the use of the decimal system in the United Kingdom. For example, my grandchildren, and indeed grown up children, do not use imperial measures; they are simply no longer taught in schools.

Archaic terms

The British Navy used the fathoms, to measure depth of water, until the 1970s. A fathom was six feet in length (see below). It was clumsy to use where absolute accuracy was required and hindered the internationalisation of navigation. It was later replaced by metres on all maritime charts.

1 fathom = 6 feet = 1.83 metres

Weight was measured in stones or pounds. The former term is used in the book.

$$1 \text{ stone} = 6.35 \text{ kgs}$$
$$160 \text{ stone} = 1 \text{ UK Ton}$$
$$143 \text{ stone} = 1 \text{ USA ton}$$

Terms still in use

Wind speed is described in this book in the Beaufort Scale. It was invented by Sir Francis Beaufort in 1805 and adopted by the British Navy in the 1830s. It is still used today. However, I am aware that in many countries wind is measured in metres or kilometres per second.

The Beaufort Scale has thirteen levels ranging from zero (dead calm) to twelve (hurricane force, 188 km/hour and above).

In this story, Force 4 is mentioned in several places, and is described by Beaufort as "gentle breeze, wind speed 12 – 19 km/hour. Large wavelets and flags extended".

Distance at sea is measured in nautical miles. One nautical mile = 1.15 miles = 1.85 kilometres.

Boat speed is measured internationally in knots. One knot = 1 nautical mile per hour.

Imperial "foot" is 30.48 centimetres.

Glossary

Approved school – A type of residential institution in the United Kingdom to which young people could be sent by a court, usually for committing an offence. They were in use until 1969.

Borstal – A youth detention centre in use in England until 1982

PE – Physical Education

Chapter 1

EARLY MAY, 1940
ST JOHN'S APPROVED SCHOOL

April had just turned into May. The head physical education instructor, Fraser Tasker, deemed that the sea would still be cold enough for the boys' weekly swim to be more punishment than pleasure.

Three teenagers sat side by side on the stoney foreshore, facing the sullen sea. Sullen because the school's residential buildings shaded the grey-blue watery surface from the south wind and the sea was always lifeless at full tide. Lifeless, that is, apart from where three score or more youths in black shorts were splashing and generally causing mayhem while a small number of others were trying to swim. Mayhem, because this was the only time during the week when the instructors did not, or rather could not, impose their harsh authority to limit the risk of losing control of the forty or so errant youths under their charge. The result was the chaotic burst of released energy now to be seen a few feet from the shoreline. But the water sport had a sinister side, for it was often then that, in the salty spume and spray thrown up by the activity, away from the gaze of authority, some scores were settled, and the punishments decreed by the "Dad" were meted out.

Two of the sitting boys were intently observing the aquatics. However, Pearson, the one sitting in the middle, was gazing at the sea beyond the swimmers. He had never been in a boat, but he held a fond notion that to be afloat would give him the freedom he had hardly ever experienced on land.

There was a crunching sound from behind the three. They knew that trouble was coming and snatched at their white vests to get them off before Mr Tasker reached them.

"Get into that bloody water now!" growled the tall, well-built man wearing a training overall.

"I knows how to swim already, even underwater," said Pearson.

His utterance was pushing at the limits of insolence that the man would tolerate, and the youth knew that.

The instructor raised the cane he was carrying and sliced it through the air. Quite intentionally, he did not hit the speaker, just whipping his bamboo close enough to remind the youth, what pain it could cause.

"Then get into that ruddy sea, Pearson, and show the others how to do it."

Tasker knew well that Pearson could swim and indeed, in his opinion, it was probably the only thing the boy did excel at.

The surly trio shuffled over the shifting stones towards the waiting sea at a pace that demonstrated their audacity to other boys watching but just kept within the limits which, if infringed, might have caused them to feel the sting of the cane.

Pearson knew how to judge where these limits were, for he had been in the approved school for longer than his companions, and before this one, when optimistic adults still had hope that their charity might save him from a life of crime, he had learnt the tricks of survival in a brutal environment.

So as not to be heard, the tall boy on Pearson's left side leaned towards him and whispered. "What are you goin' to do about Squealer Wheeler, Dad?"

Pearson looked round to see how close the teachers were and, deciding that they were not within earshot, he glanced up at his tall companion and hissed, "When Tasker ain't watching, grab him by the balls, Lofty, and I want to hear the little bugger scream."

"OK, Dad. You reckon that's enough to stop him grassing on us?"

"It'll do for now. But I want you to give Smithy a lesson too."

"Yeah, he's gettin' too cheeky and I reckon he's started to sell fags. That's your pitch. What you want us to do?"

"Give his nose a good prod. I want to see blood in the water."

Pearson was "Dad" in the school. The undisputed leader of all the boys. It was a title earned by brutality and held by the fear it instilled in others. He had learnt the importance of this status the hard way, in another place, when he was younger. On his arrival at St Johns Approved School, when he was transferred from a more lenient institution, he wasted no time to identify the then "Dad". The brutish incumbent was always flanked by his two lieutenants. They carried out his orders and protected him.

In the washroom, on the first morning of his stay, Pearson had noticed that there was an unoccupied hand basin next to the one with a running tap where the Dad was wiping a flannel across his face. The new boy took the adjacent basin and slowly washed his own face, glancing frequently at his neighbour, waiting for his chance. As the leader bent over his basin to rinse, Pearson leapt up, pounced on top of him and, with all his weight, smashed the Dad's open mouth into the edge of the porcelain. As the scream subsided, it was clear from the blood and the splintered teeth that Dad would not respond. He tried to stand up, wobbled, and then crashed to the floor. His two lieutenants looked at each other in dismay and first one, and then the other, offered their allegiance to Pearson.

"Come on, out of the water, all of you!" shouted Tasker.

The other two instructors chivvied the slower boys, waving their canes at them.

"Put your plimsoles and vests on and stand in line!" Tasker shouted again as he pointed to where they should gather.

"Ain't we going to get dressed, sir?" Pearson called to the man.

"Not yet, Pearson, you are all going to get dried off first by doing the 'circuit'." There were groans and muted protests from those who had heard. These died away as a message was passed amongst the crowd. As one, they all turned to watch. One of their number, helped along by another, was wailing even more loudly than the sound of the crunching shingle as he painfully progressed up the slope. Another was wiping blood from his nose, using his white vest.

"Don't use your vest, Smith. It'll stop soon enough. What's wrong with you, Wheeler?" asked Tasker.

The wailing ceased and a weak voice said, "I got hurt, sir." There were sniggers among those in the know.

Addressing the boy helping Wheeler, he said, "Take the damned softie to the sick bay."

Tasker stretched to his full height and addressed the boys.

"We are doing the circuit now instead of this afternoon. After your midday meal, the Head wants to see all of those who will be seventeen this year."

There were whisperings among the crowd. One of the boys put up his hand.

"Yes, Turner, what is it?"

Tasker showed impatience, regarding Turner as a nuisance who did not deserve his response.

"I don't know if I am seventeen. Mum never said how old I was when I come here."

There were giggles and comments around the crowd.

"All right, you idiot, we'll talk about it later. Quiet, everyone. We are going to run round the usual circuit. Mr Wright will lead; Mr Scott will be in the middle. I will be at the back to discourage any loiterers. Now, get in line."

The "circuit" was the standard cross country running track used three or four times a week by the school. While most of the boys' time was spent on practical courses in carpentry, painting, and decorating and plumbing, PE was seen as the way for them to work off youthful energy and thus minimise their inclination to cause disruption. The route the run took led first across a main road and then along a lane that passed the back gardens of a housing estate. The properties were separated from the lane by a wire link fence that was about adult waist height. At the end of the lane, runners had to climb over a stile before following a circular trail through a wood, which eventually returned to the stile and led them back to the school.

While the staff recognised the value of running the circuit, it was not a popular duty for teachers. There were multiple possibilities for boys to abscond unless they were kept "bunched up" and under the view of the three adults. Neither was the activity popular with those who lived in the housing estate, for the inhabitants felt vulnerable about the attentions of the passing delinquents.

The boys stood in the line, waiting for the order to start and the customary warning from Mr Tasker.

"Boys, let me remind you of two things", he began, despite the low level of murmurings and moanings from the line.

"Firstly, it is forbidden for you to talk to members of the public or make rude noises."

Someone in the line made the sound of a fart. The ensuing giggling quickly died down when the instructor raised his cane.

"Secondly, I will remind you that in all approved schools, the standard punishment for a boy who absconds is eight strokes of the cane on a clothed backside. We, in this school, interpret this to mean that thin PE shorts constitute a clothed backside. Mr Wright will lead the run, and Mr Scott will be in the middle."

There was some chattering before Mr Tasker shouted, "Ready, Mr Wright? There is a teacher waiting to hold up the traffic for you."

"Ready, Mr Tasker."

"Off you go."

Pearson was, for reasons best known to himself, directly behind Mr Wright, at the front of the line, together with his two henchmen, as they crossed the road and started running past the gardens. As ever, on a Monday, the clothes lines were festooned with the weekly wash of the occupants of the houses. And as ever, as soon as the boys caught sight of women and girls' underwear hanging out to dry, there were whoops and wolf whistles from the passing adolescents. Pearson paid no attention, for he was looking for other things.

As they neared the stile, he deliberately slowed down to get the best view possible of the garden of the second to last house before they would climb over and into the woods.

Mr Wright, (known between the boys as "Ticker" because of the relationship between getting something right and a tick), slowed and turned. Running on the spot he said, "Come on, Pearson, keep up."

As he spoke, there was a commotion further back in the line. The runners had stopped and were gathering around one who had fallen to the ground.

Ticker hesitated; clearly Mr Scott needed assistance, but did he dare to leave Pearson and the others at the front of the queue, unsupervised?

"Pearson, I'm trusting you to stay here and wait. No funny business, right?"

"No, sir, you can trust me", said Pearson.

The boy stepped over to the garden fence, felt how secure it was and then craned to see if there really was a gap between the houses that opened on to the street. There was. And the bicycle was still there, propped against the wall as always. Most important of all, the blue engineer's boiler suit was in amongst the drying laundry as it was every Monday. He turned to check where Mr Wright was and saw the teacher coming towards him.

"There, sir, I told you that you could trust me!"

"Um, yes, well done, young Pearson. Good man. Come on, we are off again."

Lofty, one of his lieutenants who had his back to Mr Wright, looked at Pearson and clearly mimed, "Ass licker." Pearson grinned and winked. He was satisfied with the test of his diversion plan and the useful reconnaissance.

Following the teacher, the line of runners, one after another, started climbing over the stile.

During the run, out of Ticker's earshot, his second companion, Sid, asked, "You really goin' to make a breakout?"

"That depends on how things go for me. But I have a plan ready."

"Yeah, I noticed what you were doin'."

"Keep it to yourself, I don't want Squealer finding out."

Later, while the boys were in the canteen having their main meal of the day, several members of staff were meeting in the headmaster's office.

The man sitting behind a large mahogany desk, wearing a white collar, which denoted him as a man of the cloth, spoke.

"Well, gentlemen, the time has come for us to make recommendations as to the futures of those of our flock who will reach seventeen this year. They will be leaving us at the end of this term. Since we are at war with Germany, the situation and options open to us are different from those in peace time."

"Headmaster, before we begin, can I mention to all that I have received my call-up papers. I will be leaving the school in June to join the Army as a PE instructor."

"That is indeed bad news for the school, Mr Tasker, and a great loss to our boys. I fear that several others of you will eventually be called to the colours.

"Now, to the matter in hand. I would remind you that there are three main options open to us. Boys who have shown little progress or redemption should move to Borstal Prison where they will live with other young men offenders. The second, newer option is to recommend the boys to a branch of the armed services for training. Obviously, because of their histories, the choice would be limited to joining the army or, in the case of very able boys, the navy might be possible.

"And finally, where a boy has shown exceptional abilities in practical skills and no inclination to difficult behaviour, we can in some instances recommend that he should be released, and we will help him to find a job."

There was a short silence while those present considered the headmaster's words.

He spoke again. "So, let's start with the boy who has been with us longest: Pearson. Mr Tasker, you see much of him because of his sporting talents. What do you think?"

"Thank you, Headmaster. Yes, a boy who is quite talented at some sports, in particular swimming. But let's be frank. Though he has shown no tangible academic progress he has shown a great aptitude for gangsterism. We all know that he is the leader of the boys, that he and his pals control them. And we do nothing about that because his clever influence over them helps the staff to keep order. We don't question the fact that he undoubtedly illegally obtains cigarettes from outside the school and has a monopoly in selling them to the boys. I am sure too that he is responsible for selling and distributing some very racy illustrated literature which the cleaners have drawn to our attention."

There was a loud harrumph from the headmaster. It was clear to all that Mr Tasker, knowing that he would shortly be leaving the school, dared to speak the unspoken about the school underworld.

Mr Tasker continued, "He is a strong contender for Borstal."

There was an uneasy silence in the room. It was broken by Mr Wright.

"Come, come, Mr Tasker, the boy has his good sides. I find him cooperative, and I have to say, I also find him trustworthy. Don't forget too, that he has passed his first aid course."

"He is also clever with his hands and has done some good work in my classes," Mr Jenkins, the metalwork teacher, quickly added.

Five minutes later, after further discussion, the headmaster concluded the matter.

"Then we have a majority who recommend that I offer Pearson the choice of our help to join the army or to be transferred to Borstal."

There were some sounds of agreement.

"Then let us proceed. Who shall we consider next?"

A few days later, as the boys were clearing their plates and cutlery, and taking them for cleaning by those on washing-up duty, Mr Tasker's loud voice commanded silence.

"As I mentioned some days ago, all boys who are or will be seventeen this year will be seeing the head. Would these boys gather in the recreation area and wait outside the office entrance until they are called in, one at a time."

There was a buzz of conversation as they all departed the canteen. Outside, the required boys sorted themselves out from the others into a group, as directed. They were followed by Mr Tasker, who carried a clipboard in one hand and his cane in the other. He pushed his way through the crowd and climbed the three steps to the office entrance, then turned and faced the boys.

"Each of you are due to leave St John's at the end of the summer term. The headmaster will have a discussion with you, individually, about your future."

"I told you, Lofty, that's what it's all about," whispered Pearson.

"That's a relief, I thought we were in trouble."

"That's enough, quiet, everyone. First on my list is Pearson. Come with me, lad."

The teacher led the way through the office and knocked on the headmaster's door.

"Come in!" shouted a voice. Pearson recognised the sound well. He had listened to the whining tone of the Reverend Baxter hour after hour, week after week, and indeed year after year as the man submitted the boys to sermon after sermon on Sundays.

Ticker was already in the room standing in a corner as Tasker led Pearson in.

"Stand in front of the headmaster's desk, Pearson. No hands in pockets."

"Ah, Pearson. Mr Tasker has told me of your prowess in swimming. I am so pleased to hear that you channel your energies into such a commendable activity."

The boy shrugged his shoulders and looked uncomfortable.

There was a momentary silence while the head surveyed a paper in front of him.

"You have been with us a long time, Pearson."

He fiddled with some more papers.

"Four and half years, sir."

"Ah yes, er so it is, I see here."

He paused again as he read.

"You have a violent past. Why did you attack your father with a coal shovel?"

"He weren't my father, he was my stepdad and not really that 'cause he never married my mum before she died."

"Nevertheless, Mr Charlton was kind enough to continue to provide for you."

"Provide! He never provided me with more than the scars of his belt buckle I still have on my back."

The headmaster sensed that the boy's tone was somewhat more aggressive than he was able to deal with. He looked at Tasker. The teacher took the hint and said, "Pearson, remember who you are speaking to and apologise."

The boy's instinct was to kick out, but he restrained himself, for he had good reason to be at peace with those who would decide his future.

"Sorry, sir, that was wrong of me."

"Quite so, Pearson. Your record shows that you have also been in court to answer theft and breaking and entering charges."

Quietly and slowly, Pearson controlled himself, then said, "It's true, sir, but what it don't say in the records, sir, is that I was stealing to get food for me and my little brother. Charlton was away for days at a time and left us alone, I was just thirteen."

"And the break-in?"

"Yeah, well that was wrong of me I know. I could see the kids' toys through the window, things that I wanted my brother to have. I thought the house was empty when I picked the lock."

"You picked the lock?"

"Yeah, well Charlton taught me some useful things."

At this comment, Tasker could not avoid looking at the other teacher and grinning.

"And you attacked the owner of the house?"

"Na, well I just give him a little poke on the chin and scarpered. I never meant for him to fall over and hurt himself."

"Are you a better person now, Pearson? What have these four and a half years done for you?"

"Oh, yeah, sir. I'm a better person, I really am. I learnt a lot here, especially metal work. I hope that I can get a job with an engineering firm when I leave here, sir."

"That brings us to the point of this meeting. Your future."

Before the head could continue, Pearson interrupted him.

"I really want to make an honest living working with metal. Please help me."

The Reverend Baxter gave another harrumph, indicating his annoyance.

"My staff have considered your case and recommended to me that you have not sufficiently repaid your debt to society. As such, the obvious place for you to be after leaving here is at a borstal."

Pearson gasped, but before he could protest, the speaker continued.

"However, we all recognise that you have some useful talents, not least, um...how should I put it? Yes, your organisational skills."

Again, the head hastened to continue before the boy had a chance to react.

"I have agreed with the staff that you would make a soldier. Therefore, we have decided to offer you the option of joining the army, instead of going to borstal."

Pearson tried to control himself as he said, "I don't want to join no army."

"Pearson, we are at war. The army needs all the recruits it can get. I am sure that there will be a branch where you can develop your metal working skills. So, I will repeat our generous offer. You can choose between further incarceration, in a borstal, or the opportunity to join the army."

Pearson stepped forward and banged his fist on the desk.

"I said, I ain't gonna join no fuckin' army."

The head, who had quickly pushed his chair back when he saw the boy moving towards him, endeavoured to stand up as Tasker and Wright grabbed Pearson and dragged him away from the desk.

The dismayed vicar waved his hand towards the door, beckoning the men to remove the recalcitrant.

Stuttering, he said, "Gentleman, I leave you to deal with this."

The distraught Pearson knew what this meant.

• • • • • • • • ● • • • • • • • • •

The three teenagers sat on the stoney foreshore watching the antics of the boys in the sea. The minority, the would-be swimmers, were trying to evade the chaotic majority who were generally larking about.

"We'd better get into the water before Tasker gets here," said Lofty.

"Hang on a bit, I want to tell you something before we go down there," Pearson responded.

"Go on."

"I've been thinking, if only Baxter had offered me to join the navy, I might have said yes."

"Why?"

"I've never been in a boat but really like the idea of it."

"Why don't you go back to him and ask?"

"Na, Lofty. Can you see him letting me get into his office again?"

Pearson laughed as he said, "You should have seen the old bugger, I scared him right and proper. No, he wants me in the borstal now."

"You should have accepted the army, it beats borstal," said Sid, the other lieutenant.

"Yeah, what you got against the army?" asked Lofty.

"Plenty, more than enough."

There was a silence. Pearson could not show the emotion he felt without appearing weak in front of the other two. He could not betray the hate he had of the army uniform. A uniform he associated with the different men wearing it when they came to visit his mother at night-time. A time when he was locked in a cupboard under the stairs until they had gone.

"So, what you gonna do then?" asked Lofty.
"You know about my plan?
"Yeah."
Well first time we get a circuit run on a Monday morning, I'm off. You know the help I need from you, don't you?"
"Yeah, we'll back you up, won't we, Sid?"
The sound of crunching stones behind them galvanised them into quickly pulling their white vests off.

Chapter 2

TUESDAY MORNING, 28ᵀᴴ MAY 1940

For the time of year, it was a chilly morning. The day before, the day when Pearson's year group normally had their first cross country run of the week, the weather had been very wet, and the activity was postponed. The air was still damp, and the low cloud seemed to threaten that the day would not be dry for long.

"Come on, Pearson, keep up with me. You others, keep up with Pearson. Quick, get across the road," called Ticker.

Pausing briefly to look at the procession of boys in black shorts, white vests and wearing black plimsols, Pearson noted with satisfaction that Lofty and Sid were about halfway back, quite close to Mr Scott but just behind him.

The runners entered the lane. It was clear that the laundry day had also been postponed to today. The washing lines were full of varied clothes and sheets. There was very little wind, so the items hung listlessly, the housewives in the street optimistically hoping that the sun might break through. It was not long before some runners spotted girls' underclothes, even though they had been hung as discreetly as possible, behind garments of less interest to the teenage boys. The customary whoops and whistles sounded until Mr Scott slowed, stopped, and then turned in a vain attempt to identify the source of the noise. He resumed running until there was a loud shout, which Pearson, some distance further forward, knew was the signal for Lofty to punch the nearest runner and for Sid to do the same. The middle of the line erupted into a melee of fists flying and oaths being shouted.

At the head of the line, Ticker had the same dilemma as he had once had several weeks before. He looked at Pearson and said, "Stay here and don't let anyone get past. I'm depending on you!"

"Of course, sir," Pearson answered.

As soon as Ticker's back was turned and he was making his way back along the line to help Mr Scott, Pearson took a short run towards the fence, put his left hand on a post, and vaulted over into the garden. Two bedsheets obscured him as he reached up and pulled off the four pegs holding the boiler suit. It was heavier than he had expected as it was still quite wet. He quickly opened the front of the one-piece overalls and tried to put his foot in. The trouser legs did not open! The suit was so wet that the heavy cloth was clinging and making it difficult to put his foot in! He hopped on one leg, desperately trying to drag the heavy cloth over his foot.

"Bugger, the plimsoles catch on the cloth, hadn't expected that," he mumbled to himself as he realised that he would have to sit on the ground to solve the problem.

The whole thing was taking longer than he had expected. He tried to stay calm. He knew that his disappearance might be detected at any moment.

"Oh damn, there's Ticker walking back up the lane to the front of the runners. No! This can't go wrong; I planned it so well!" he said to himself.

Pearson stood up. Hiding behind a bed sheet as he was doing up the buttons, he peeped out to see what was happening.

"Where's Pearson, where is the damned boy?" Ticker demanded of those nearest.

First one, then several, pointed towards the stile.

"I told him to wait here, damn him. Come on, he's probably waiting in the woods."

Pearson peered out between two sheets and watched as the line of runners continued past him. He grinned as he saw Lofty's bloody nose and several boys with torn vests. Finally, Tasker passed him.

Pearson paused for a while and then crept up the garden towards the house. He could hear a baby crying inside. "Hopefully, that will keep the mother occupied," he thought.

There was no cover to hide behind once he had come to the end of the washing line. He took a deep breath and sprinted, as much as the wet overalls would allow, towards the bicycle. When he had reached it, he crouched down next to the wall of the house to examine the bike.

It was locked! There was a chain draped round the back mudguard and through the wheel. He examined the padlock. "Should be easy," he thought. He put his hand in his pocket to get his lock pick.

"Bugger!" he mumbled to himself. "I can't get my hand into my shorts pocket without undoing all the buttons on the top of the overall."

He was losing valuable time even though he was sure that as soon as Ticker realised that he was missing, it would take at least half an hour for news to get back to the office, probably a lot longer because the teacher could not just abandon the other boys and run back to report that he had absconded.

Pearson writhed and twisted to get his hand under the wet overall and into his shorts pocket. He pulled out the skeleton key, one of his metal working successes, though not one that was ever seen by the teacher.

The padlock was quickly opened, and Pearson carefully lifted the chain away from the wheel, trying to stop it rattling. He did up the buttons and stood up. The bike was a good height for him. He mounted and headed for the road towards Newport. He had long anguished about the best route. If he took the minor country roads there was less chance of running into a police patrol, but the route would be longer. He had decided that even though there would be more traffic, and possibly searchers, on the main road, they would be looking for a boy in black shorts and a white vest, not a workman in overalls. Nevertheless, Pearson wanted to keep well away from Newport, in the centre of the island, before people started looking for him. It was there that there was most danger of police patrols. He hoped too that those searching would assume that he would try to get to the nearest harbour, Yarmouth, from where he could escape to the mainland. That was in the opposite direction to his planned destination – Cowes.

It was over five years since Pearson had last ridden a bicycle and at first, he cycled slowly and very carefully. After a while he felt assured enough to increase his speed. When vehicles coming towards him passed, he put his head down, just in case his description had been circulated. As regards the overalls, the woman in the house would probably not find that they were missing until later in the day when she took the laundry in. Perhaps it would take even longer for the theft of the bike to be discovered.

Pearson was elated that things were now looking positive and, so far, his plan had worked, but despite this he also had a growing sense of unease. For over four years, he had lived in the school. Life there was harsh and brutal, but paradoxically, he had total reliance on the security it provided. He had never had to worry about food, clothes, or other features of the real world. He was institutionalised. Now he was on his own and would have to live by his wit and not according to the dictates of school authority.

Although it was not yet midday, he was beginning to feel very hungry and was becoming aware that while the idea of freedom was attractive, he had thought no further than escaping, with little forethought about practicalities. The growing realisation that he would have to fend for himself with no money, perhaps for days, was beginning to occupy his mind.

He had been cycling for some time when he reached a small village, where he slowed down and stopped. In a side road he saw a village shop about fifty yards away. Outside was a rusty van with the back doors open. As he watched, he saw an old man, wearing a brown apron, going in and out of the shop, unloading trays of bread from the van and taking them inside. The speed he was working indicated to

Pearson that there was probably enough time to grab a loaf from the van while the man was in the shop. He cycled closer and waited, like a hunting animal ready to pounce. The baker came out of the shop and slid out another tray, then lifted it slowly and walked back through the open shop door.

Pearson pushed hard on the pedals and accelerated towards the van. He arrived there just as the baker reappeared.

"Careful, lad, you'll hurt yourself. You come to get bread?"

Pearson was furious with himself for misjudging how long the deed would take. Thinking quickly, he said, "Yeah, but I forgot my money.""I'll not make a living from you then," said the baker looking the boy up and down.

"You working on the bomb shelter in the village?"

"Yeah."

"Tell you what, I got a couple of yesterday's loaves. You can have one of 'em.""Oh, thanks, mister."

The baker leant far into the van and then turned, holding up a loaf.

"Here you are, son, and be more careful on that bike.""Thanks, mister, thanks a lot."

Pearson put the bread under his arm and cycled back towards the main road. He stopped and looked over his shoulder to make sure that the baker was not looking to see which way he turned and then continued his journey, looking for an opening into the woods, out of sight of other travellers, where he might stop and eat some bread. After a while he spotted an overgrown track leading to a small copse. He got off and wheeled his bike into the wood, then put it against a tree before breaking the loaf open and eating most of it. After a short rest, much refreshed, he resumed his journey.

As he neared the island's capital, the now very wary cyclist found that the level of traffic was increasing, though most of it consisted of military vehicles. Suddenly, he heard a bell ringing loudly. It was a black Wolseley trying to overtake an army lorry coming towards him. As it did so, he saw that the sign on the roof said "POLICE". Pearson put his head down low and moved as close as he could to the verge of the road as the car rushed past him, heading in the direction from which he had travelled. He gave a sigh of relief and chuckled, saying to himself, "They're going the wrong way and they ain't looking for someone in overalls yet."

The road he had been travelling on was heading east; now at a junction, he stopped. The road signs had been removed to make things as difficult as possible for an enemy in the event of an invasion. Pearson considered his two options, left or right. Looking down the road on the left, he could see rows of army huts with lots of traffic coming and going. There was also what looked like a prison. He turned right, hoping to find a better way up the river, where the roads were not so busy. He had sped halfway down a steep hill when he caught sight of the Medina River.

"Hell, I've gone the wrong way. This leads into Newport!"

It was too late to change his mind, but he took the first left turning he could find to avoid the town centre. The road led to the harbour. He cycled slowly under a railway bridge and then paused to look at the scene in front of him. It was a busy, noisy place, but as far as he could see, there were no police in evidence. He cautiously cycled along the quay, stopping now and again to look at small ships being unloaded. Most used a crane on the ship to lift boxes and other goods out of their holds. One small crane on the quay, with a round roof, was unloading timber. From there the wood was being put on a trailer drawn by a cart horse. He watched as the trailer passed him, making its way to a very large shed. Further on, there was a pile of crates and boxes. These were being loaded on to army lorries that were queueing for their turn to pick up goods. Close by there was the slow "pomp", "pomp", "pomp", sound from a ship's engine.

Pearson came to his senses; the fascinating sights and sounds were diverting him from making good his escape. Nevertheless, he found it difficult to detach himself. He plucked up courage and rode up to a bench where an old man was sitting, watching the goings on around him while smoking his pipe.

He looked up at the boy and asked, "What you doin', nipper?"

"Ah, well just riding my bike."

"Lad like you should be workin' here, not watchin'. I started here when I was twelve years."

"Where do the ships go?"

"Depends on the cargo, but most often Southampton, though these days more frequently to Portsmouth for military cargoes."

"Will they leave today?"

The old man took a long draw on his pipe and then slowly said, "Some will, some won't. Shouldn't wonder if one or two catch the ebb tide and then moor in Cowes until nightfall. 'Taint a good idea to sail the Solent in daylight what with all them Bossche planes about."

The boy decided that he had lavished enough precious time asking questions, though the information was of great interest to him.

"Gotta go, bye."

"'Ere boy, look there's one of the boats just goin' now."

The pulsing "pomp", "pomp" was changing its rhythm and getting faster.

"Why's he going? Bit late in the day, ain't it?"

"You see that post over there, it shows the depth of water. Look, just on six foot. We're on neaps, so it ain't going to get any higher than that."

He pulled a pocket watch out of his waistcoat and looked at it. Yeah, 'tis four o'clock. High tide is about now. The captain's goin' to use the ebb tide to help him down the river."

"What's neaps?"

"Don't know much do you, lad? That's when the difference between high and low tides is the least."

The old sailor pointed his pipe at the ship, which was slowly being manoeuvred around in the narrow river, to face downstream to the north.

"That's the *Bee*, goin' to Cowes I fancy, to pick up cargo."

The old man waved his pipe at the ship and shouted, "That's the way to do it, Ben!"

A man standing behind a large wheel, in the small building towards the back of the ship, waved in appreciation of the comment.

"Where will he go, then?" asked the boy.

"More likely Portsmouth, I should say."

Pearson watched for a few moments as the ship, towing a rowing boat, headed away from the quay. He raised a hand in farewell to the man on the crate and then got on his bike to climb a steep hill out of the harbour. It was too much of a challenge for the now-weary youth. Half-way up, out of breath, he got off and pushed the bike the rest of the way. When he got to the top and came to a junction, it was easy for him to sense which way was north and would lead him to East Cowes. He got on again and started pedalling.

It was mid-afternoon when the cyclist passed through the town and reached the end of the road and the mouth of the river. Avoiding a busy place where a ferry came in, he found his way to another road, which was parallel with the river, and cycled along it. There was a long row of similar buildings with pointed, sloping roofs, some with doors open. Looking in, he could see what he guessed was some kind of factory. He passed a pub called the Victoria Tavern and soon after, on his right, found a small lane leading down to the river's edge. He followed it. The scene before him was one of great activity. There were small boats plying from one side to the waterway to the other, some carrying people, others heaps of goods. Most were being rowed; others were under power. However, it was the extraordinary scene on the far side of the river that held his attention. There, alongside a wharf, in the shadow of a huge crane, was a massive ship. All over the hull there were men working, suspended on small platforms hanging from ropes fastened to the topside of the ship. They seemed to be painting the vessel dark grey. As they laboured on the outside, there was an almost continuous sound of rivets being banged into metal on the topside.

Pearson stood his bike against a wall and walked closer to the river to get a better view. As he rounded the end, he was startled by a voice. There, sitting on a makeshift bench made of a plank supported by two piles of bricks, were two men in overalls. Each was cradling a brown bottle in one hand and a pipe in the other.

"What you doin' 'ere, lad?" asked one.

The boy tried to recover from his shock by replying, "I, I wanted to see the river."

"'ear that, Harry, he wanted to see the river," said the man as he raised the bottle to his lips.

"Well, take a good look and then bugger off," said the other. "Can't a man even get his tea before night shift in peace?"

"Yeah, yeah of course I will," stuttered Pearson. "But…tell me, what ship is that over there?"

"That, son, is, or is soon to be, a minesweeper. A Hunt class minesweeper. We moved her across to the other side to Theta wharf, where the company has another factory for fittin' out ships," said the less aggressive man. "And it ain't the first one JS Whites have built here, nor will it be the last. There's plenty of work for ship builders in wartime."

"But that'n is a littlun, most often 'tis destroyers we builds, ain't it, Stan?"

"Yeah, there was them two we built for the Polish navy afore the war."

Pearson was suddenly aware of the purpose of his day: he should be avoiding people, not getting involved with them.

"Bye, then," he said as he turned to go back to his bike. As he did so, his attention was caught by the movement of a black ship coming down river. He paused to watch it. The men had gone back to chatting and no longer seemed interested in him. He almost blurted out what he was thinking to himself, "That's the ship I saw in Newport, it says *Bee* on the front."

As the vessel came closer, he suddenly realised that his plan had gone seriously wrong. It was slowing down alongside a space on the same wharf that the warship occupied and there was someone there waiting as if to take the *Bee*'s mooring line.

"Oh no!" the boy said to himself, "I'm on the wrong bloody side of the river!"

Pearson stood transfixed, staring at the vessel docking on the other side of the flowing water. He was furious with himself for having assumed that the ship would berth on the east side of the river.

His plan to put the sea between him and the school now seemed an impossible scheme. He thought for a while and then decided to take the risk of making the two men angry.

Walking back round the end of the wall and about to ask the men a question, the aggressive one blurted, "Gor blimey, Stan, he's back! Who are you anyways?"

"Sorry, sir, I'm new to the island. Can you tell me how I can cross the river?"

"Why don't you swim? That'd be a sight for sore eyes to watch with the tide runnin' as it is," said Harry.

They both laughed, then Stan said, "There's a ferry what crosses the Medina, just down by the town. It'll cost you a penny. That's the price one-way."

"I'm obliged to you, sir," said the boy as he left and quickly went back to his bike.

Now he had another problem: he had no money. He considered his situation for a few moments and then said to himself, "I've got to take a chance, otherwise today has been a waste of time."

Pearson cycled past the factory and back to where he had seen a crowd waiting for a ferry. He got off the bike and sat on a nearby bench, watching people assembling and waiting for a vessel that was being pulled across the river on chains. The boy was now very hungry, thirsty, tired, and extremely nervous; his situation was really vulnerable, especially if his description had been circulated. What would happen if he embarked on the ferry without paying? Surely, he would be held by the ticket collector and the police called.

The ferry reached land, and as soon as the passengers had disembarked, those who had been waiting swarmed aboard. There were people with bikes, prams, and pushchairs and one in a wheelchair.

His nerve broke. He did not dare to risk going aboard. He sat watching, feeling completely helpless and not knowing what to do. He tried to clear his head, but he was like a fish out of water. For almost his total life, he had had to do as others told him. Apart from his "business activities", others had always decided for him. Others dictated what he should wear, what he should eat, when he should sleep and wake. Everything was decided by others. He never was allowed, nor did he need, to make decisions. He had thought that freedom from the approved school would be a wonderful experience which would give him many possibilities. He had planned it for many months, but now he just did not know what to do. He put his head in his hands and tried to think logically.

Suddenly, Pearson was jolted by a loud wailing sound that pierced the air. He looked up; the ferry had gone. Looking round, it seemed that the noise came from the direction of the factory he had recently passed. Then it stopped. Shortly after, some bikes appeared from the same direction. Within seconds there were more and very shortly, there were literally hundreds of men and women on bicycles hurrying down the road towards the ferry.

"It must be the end of the shift!" he said to himself.

He quickly got onto his bike and joined the mass of people waiting for the ferry to return. To his great relief, he saw that he blended in very well with the crowd, most of them were in blue overalls! But as he surveyed the crowd, he realised that he was the only young man in sight. Nearly all of the men were grey haired or balding, a sure sign that younger men must have joined the forces. The women also wore overalls. There was a lot of high-spirited noise, as the crowd were clearly pleased that their day's work was done.

After what was a very anxious wait, Pearson saw that the ferry was now making its way back across the river towards where he was standing. His multiple fear of being recognised and caught, and not having the fare, made him almost shiver with trepidation. The ferry docked and the ramp was quickly lowered to the ground, which it hit with a loud clang. The wooden gate on the ferry opened and people in working clothes streamed off, pushing bicycles.

"Here comes the night shift!" a nearby man shouted to his companion. Pearson overheard and understood that these must be on their way to the factory. The last passengers walked down the ramp and those waiting were waved to come onboard. There were two ferry crew members standing by the ramp leading up to the vessel. They were obviously overwhelmed by this new huge stream of workers eager to get to their homes after a day's work. Intending passengers gave a coin to one or other of the crew as they passed or threw one into the open leather pouches that the boatmen wore on a belt round their waists. As he passed one of the men, Pearson deliberately stumbled and said loudly, "Bugger, I dropped it!"

"Go on, I'll pick it up later," said the flustered official.

"Thanks, mate," said the boy. Then the gate was closed and the ramp raised. The vessel started moving, to the accompaniment of a loud clanking from the chain.

From where he stood, Pearson could see the quay where the *Bee* had berthed, but the ship was hidden behind the much larger vessel. However, what was apparent was that to reach the ship, he would have to go through the shipyard. This meant that he would have to find the entrance to JS Whites. The rhythm of the clanking began to get slower, and he saw the ramp beginning to descend. There was a loud thump as the metal hit the concrete slope leading up a slight hill. Passengers started moving towards the wooden gate in front of the ramp, keen to disembark. Many people had stood there for the whole passage, hoping to be off quickly. Pearson joined the throng moving forwards, pushing their bikes. He mounted and, like so many others, laboured from a standstill to ascend the slope. He had not pedalled more than a hundred yards when the long column of cyclists stopped. Ahead of him he could see an official holding up the traffic, and on the pavement beside the man there was the unmistakeable sight of a policeman's helmet. Pearson almost turned round in panic, but then he noticed a long queue of cyclists and many pedestrians moving down the hill towards him.

"Why are we stopped?" he asked a woman next to him sitting astride her bike, with her feet touching the ground.

"It's the JS Whites night shift at the Thetis wharf, they're off to work. They get's priority, lovie. This happens every bloody night darlin', they really should change the shift times."

Pearson manoeuvred his bike to get as far as could on the left-hand side of the road where he would be most obscured by the crowd. As he did so, the official let the queue he was in move forward. The boy kept his head as low as he could, occasionally glancing up to see if he had a view of the policeman. He was almost level with the officer when he realised that the policeman had his back to the ferry. He was only looking up the road, the direction the cyclists were going!

"That's it, he's there to look for someone trying to catch the ferry, coming from the direction of where the school is. He wouldn't expect me to be coming this way!" he said to himself.

As soon as Pearson got level with the gateway over which it said, "JS Whites", he turned, dismounted, and followed others through two large open wooden gates that led to a tunnel between buildings and entered the shipyard. In front of him he found a large crowd of workers queueing outside some kind of office. He stopped and watched for a while. Those with bikes were putting them into a large cycle park and then joining the queue to go through a door at one end of the building and then emerge from another at the other end. Many then returned to their cycles and unhitched the haversacks they had hung on the handlebars.

Pearson put his bike in a space and went to look through the windows of the building. Inside, he saw that the workers were putting cards into a machine, waiting for a few seconds, then pulling the cards out again before leaving.

"You clocked on yet?" a voice from behind him asked.

Pearson turned round. There, behind him, was the same official who had been directing traffic.

"Er…yeah. Just going to get my bag."

The boy hurried to the bike shed. He waited a moment, watching more cyclists arriving. Their bags all looked very much the same, army style khaki canvas haversacks, but some were bulging more than others and a number had a telltale screw top bottle top sticking out. As his chosen victim left to clock in, Pearson waited a few seconds and then grabbed the bag. He quickly walked off through an alley by the building, towards the harbour, looking for a hiding place where he could have his first meal since the stale loaf.

Chapter 3

TUESDAY MORNING, 28ᵀᴴ MAY 1940

Ben Bainbridge looked into the mirror over the sink in the kitchen and used the scissors, intended for other purposes, to trim his moustache. He'd had his weekly shave the day before, so today he just washed his face and combed his hair while he was waiting for his turn to use the lavatory in the garden lean-to, when his sister Mae would vacate it. Beside him, his widowed sister, Amy, was frying some bacon and bread. She was one of the tens of thousands of women still grieving for a husband lost in the Great War. Although it was no longer expected, she still tended to dress in black clothes.

"Move over, Ben, you'll get splattered by the fat."

"Can you do a couple of sausages and some bread and drippin' sandwiches for me to take for mid-day meal? We'll have a fry-up on board this evenin.'" "Where are you going to, Uncle Ben?" asked Molly, Amy's twenty-three-year-old daughter.

"A bit unusual today, love. Gotta unload the timber we brought in yesterday and then catch the tide to Cowes to load up at JS Whites."

"Whites? What do you load there?" asked Molly.

"Twenty ton of iron plate. We gotta take it to Portsmouth Dockyard."

"Why do they need iron plate on the mainland?"

"They don't, Molly. 'Tis JS Whites what needs the plate to be galvanised. It can't be done 'ere. They need it for the warship they just launched, for the deck."The door opened and Mae stepped into the kitchen from the outside yard. Ben held the door for her and then left.

"It'll be June in four days. It doesn't feel like it. The privy is freezing," she said, turning on the one tap over the sink to wash her hands.

"You've forgotten what it was like in January," laughed Molly.

"We need another candle out there and some more paper."

"Molly, can you lay the table for breakfast?" asked Amy. Her comment was accompanied by a bout of coughing.

"Yes, but I have to rush, I have to be at the shop in twenty minutes," she answered.

"You'd better smarten yourself up a bit. You know how fussy Dabell's manager is."

"Yes, yes, 'If you want to sell clothes to smart ladies, you have to be smart yourself'. You don't need to remind me."

Amy continued, "And, Mae, you must hurry too, Miss Tyler is coming for a fitting at nine o'clock." Once more, her words were interspersed with harsh coughs.

"Can't you see to her? I need a quiet cigarette after breakfast."

Amy laughed and said, "You've got your customers, and I have mine. I've already helped you out with the fur trimming and that took half the night."

"Mum, you shouldn't work in the night. The gas light isn't bright enough; you have poor sight already."

Molly's intervention in the conversation was, as ever, her attempt to stop the two seamstresses' conversation descending into an argument, which she knew would inevitably lead to her mother having a coughing fit.

There was a bang as Ben closed the outside door to the kitchen and then a rattle as he placed a metal bucket into the Belfast sink. He stood beside Amy while he filled it with water.

"Breakfast will be ready when you have finished flushing the lav. Careful, you nearly knocked the frying pan off the stove."

Ben did not answer Amy but made an "um" noise. This was his speciality. "Um" could be used for various meanings, from the tone going lower, which signified resentful acquiescence or to a rising tone, which could mean surprise. In a house full of strong-willed women he had long ago learnt to absorb scoldings without comment, but just the right version of "um". He rolled up his sleeves as he watched the slow trickle of water filling the bucket.

Ben was fifty-four years old and unmarried. Yet on his left forearm, there was a tattoo, a heart with an arrow through it. Underneath the arrow it said, "I love Amy". Those who did not know him well sometimes joked that he seemed to be very fond of his sister, but those who had known him longer, knew that Ben's young sweetheart had that same name and that she had died of tuberculosis just a month before their wedding. So, instead of moving out of his childhood home as a married man, Ben stayed with his sisters. It was as well, for the cost of the large, rented Victorian terraced house would have been beyond the means of the women folk after his father died. As skipper of a motor barge his wages contributed to allow the household to live in a reasonably comfortable fashion.

"Come on, Mae, breakfast is ready to put on the table," called Amy. She paused as she coughed and then continued, "Molly, can you take Granny Alice her cup of tea? Tell her I'll come up soon to help her dress."

"Amy, you got to go to see the doctor about that cough. I reckon it's getting worse."

"I can't afford the time or the money, Ben. Mrs Francis has not paid me for that ball dress I made for her."

The comment was overheard.

"And there are others who still owe you, Mum,"

Ben put down the bucket and walked into the living room. He took a toby jug from the mantelpiece and turned it upside down. The contents rattled into his palm. Picking some coins, he proffered them to Amy.

"'Ere, there's five bob. You go and see the doctor."

"But that's your beer money, Ben, I can't take it."

"I gets paid on Friday, so I'll not miss my Sunday drink with the men."

"Well, thanks, Ben. I'll tell you what, give me your winter socks and I'll darn them for you, ready for when the cold weather comes."

"Um." When the hasty breakfast was over, Amy poured some more hot water into the large teapot and then said, "Ben, you'll have to fill up the bottle with your tea, I haven't time. Your nammit's in the haversack."

As ever, he looked into the bag and checked the food he had been given to eat with a drink of cold tea at midday break. He took out his flat cap and then did up the two haversack fasteners before getting his jacket from where it hung on the inside of the coal store door and putting it on. He kept the cap in his hand as, in deference to the ladies of the house, etiquette required that men's hats should not be worn indoors. As befitted his position on the ship, and with the advantage of living with two seamstresses, he wore a fine handmade bespoke waistcoat under his jacket. Across the waistcoat hung a silver chain that led into a pocket where he kept his watch. He took it out, looked at the clock on the mantlepiece and made a small adjustment to his watch so that it tallied with the clock, which was more accurate. He patted his right jacket pocket, where he always kept his tobacco and then said, "I need to buy a pouch of bacci before we sail."

Though holding a cigarette in her hand, Mae said, "You smoke too much of that stuff. Don't forget to put your badge on. You don't want the womenfolk pushing white feathers at you."

One of the problems of being in the Merchant Navy was that sailors did not wear any uniform. Men of fighting age not in uniform could be thought of being unpatriotic and unprepared to fight for their country. The tradition of the Great War, when women gave suspected cowards white feathers, still persisted, though not on the same scale. To avoid this, in this war, seamen not in the Royal Navy were issued with a lapel badge stating, "Merchant Navy".

Ben swung his haversack over his shoulder, picked up his raincoat from the hook in the passageway, and said, "Bye all. Comin' back tomorrow teatime."

There was a chorus of goodbyes as the front door swung closed. The walk to the harbour took just fifteen minutes. It was a route Ben had followed every working day since he was twelve years old, when he started working full-time on the quay, before he was strong enough to join a ship's crew. And strong sailors they had to be, for at that time, the previous *Bee* was a sailing barge. It was not until 1928, when the old wooden *Bee*, originally built at the beginning of the nineteenth century, was replaced by a steel ship with the same name.

Around the town three other men, Ben's crew, were observing similar early morning rituals. The motor barges that kept the island supplied with everything that could not be produced there, normally had a crew of three: skipper, engineer and mate. However, when there were more demanding or heavy cargoes to be shipped, an extra deckhand, the third hand, was employed.

The engineer, Ted Maynard, was the same age as Ben, but he had seen much more of the world. In July 1915, he had voyaged on a luxury liner, the Cunard's *Aquitania*, across the Mediterranean, and later he had spent time in France. But these were no holidays. The ship had assuredly once been a luxury liner, but in 1915 she was a troop ship and on it were thirty officers and 939 men of the Isle of Wight Rifles, 1/8 Battalion Hampshire Regiment. The destination was not one of the famous Mediterranean tourist hotspots, but Suvla Bay on Gallipoli, Turkey.

Ted had excelled in training and before leaving England he was quickly promoted to corporal in a machine gun unit. When the "Rifles" scrambled ashore on the crowded British beachhead, they had a day to collect rations, assemble equipment, and receive their orders before making a dash across a killing ground of open country under intensive enemy fire. Those who survived the withering Turkish fire took up position on a low hill, which was to become their home for several weeks.

After the British withdrawal from Gallipoli, Ted, now a sergeant, was transported with his unit to fight in the trenches in France. There, because of his gallantry, he was promoted to sub-lieutenant in the field of battle. Returning to the Isle of Wight in 1918, he trained as an engineer and later joined the local shipping company, Pickfords. His walk from home to Newport Harbour, dressed in a blue boiler suit, would take him ten minutes.

The *Bee*'s first mate was Alf Lowndes, and like Ben, he had been working on the Solent since he was a boy. His walk to work was somewhat longer and occasionally he was late, but his work rate rebutted any criticism of his punctuality. Today there would be a great deal of physical work shifting the heavy steel plates, so the shipping company had employed Bert Lock to work as third hand on board. He was just eighteen but had occasionally, for three years, already been working as a deckhand on different ships. In between times, he worked in the woodyard on the quay. This was his first voyage on the *Bee* and he knew that, as the least experienced member of the crew, he would get all the dirty jobs and would constantly have to work to earn the respect of the others, who had sailed together for many years.

When Ben arrived at the side of the ship, he heard a noise from on board and realised that Ted was already there. Sure enough, the engineer's head popped up from behind the engine on deck, at the mast, which was used with the derrick, the ship's crane.

"Mornin', Ted, what you doin'?"

"Hello, Ben, just splashing some grease on to the cogs. I hear that we are going to need to lift some heavy stuff at Cowes."

"Yes, that's so. As soon as the lads are on board, we'll start to get that timber out of the hold and onto the quay. High tide's just after four. As soon as the ebb starts, I want to turn the *Bee* round to face down stream. That bend on the opposite side of the river is makin' it difficult. We'll have to go ass afore a bit to get enough space. We'll walk her back about ten yards."

"Right, I'll get the engines warmed up after we has midday meal."

Ted walked to the stern and disappeared down a hatch to his undisputed domain – the engine room.

"Mornin', Bert, good to have you on board again."

"Mornin', Captain. When we going?"

"The tide will turn at about four. We'll be off soon after."

"Where to?"

"Cowes. Start getting the covers off the hold. When you've done that, off to the forecastle with you and get that fire goin'. We'll have a brew mid-mornin.'"

Bert started to remove the tarpaulin over the planks that covered the hold.

"Ah, there you are, Alf. Help Bert get the planks off. We got to get the timber cleared so that we can catch the tide after four."

"Aye, Skipper. It'll be an overnighter then?"

"Yeah, well I did warn you. We'll load up this evenin' and then leave at first light and nip across to Pompey afore the Germans wake up."

"You 'ope!"

"Um." By this time the quay had become a busy place. There were lorries jostling for access to goods being unloaded by other ships and competing with the horse-drawn trailers piled with timber, which was being off loaded and taken to the large sheds where it would be seasoned. Soon, a pile had formed on the quay by the side of the *Bee* as the cargo was discharged.

When the crew had finished their midday meal, Ben called them all together. Ted and Ben sat on the edge of the planks covering the hold, and Alf and Bert sat on the side of the ship, the gunnel.

"We got orders to pick up an urgent load from JS Whites and take it to the galvanisers in Portsmouth docks. So, we'll leave for Cowes as soon as the ebb starts."

"Do you want us to put the tarpaulin on the hold, skipper?" asked Alf.

"No, it'll only take us an hour or so to get to the wharf and the weather should stay dry. When we cast off, you two pull her back along the quay a bit till I says stop."

"Are we leaving Cowes in the dark after we've loaded?"

"No, Bert. I know it's safer from the point of view of avoiding enemy action, but since we ain't permitted to use navigation lights and there are always a lot of warship movements round Portsmouth, I decided that we should leave at first light and motor across at full speed. Had we been going to Southampton, t'would have been different."

"Better risk the Jerry planes than be run down in the dark by a British battleship," Ted added.

"How do you want us to get out of here, it's a bit tight," asked Bert.

Ben's instructions to the crew might have seemed unnecessarily complicated to listeners already conversant with the ways of the sea, since the permanent crew knew full well what to do, but Ben always explained his passage plan. Today, with a new crew member, the briefing was even more detailed than usual. The ignominy of a messy departure from berth would make a captain and crew the butt of many a joke. And it would be noted, for work always stopped briefly on the quay for many eyes to watch for potential disasters when ships berthed or left port.

"Alf, when you've pulled her back, put a long stern line on the starboard side, looped round that bollard on the quay. Keep it out of the water. And then cast off the other stern line. As we start to move, tighten up the looped stern line and let the engine take her head round to face north. Pull your line aboard, and off we go. Bert, hold an eye on the bow and keep that fender handy, just in case. If she don't turn quickish, use a pole to push the bow off the quay."

Ted, who in his mind had never really stopped being an army officer, was tempted into giving a pep talk to the men.

"There will be lots of eyes on us when we try to get out of this awkward berth, all waiting for us to make a balls-up of it. Let's do it properly and not let Ben down!"

"Um." There were nods and smiles.

As the ship turned to face north, Ben, who had the wheelhouse door open, heard a shout, "That's the way to do it, Ben!" He looked out at the owner of the voice, an old man sitting on an upturned crate who was waving his pipe towards the *Bee*. Beside him was a youth with a bicycle. The skipper smiled and waved back to his old ship mate before pulling the engine telegraph from "Stand By" to "Slow Ahead". In the engine room, Ted received the messages from the wheelhouse.

Shortly after, the telegraph rang again, this time, "Half Ahead". The "pomp", "pomp" of the engines got faster and louder as they propelled the seventy-five feet long ship through the water.

Just over an hour later, the *Bee* was moored in Cowes, behind a warship that was nearing completion and parallel to a high stack of square metal plates. Workmen were waiting on the quay to help load them into the *Bee*'s hold.

Chapter 4

TUESDAY EVENING, MAY 28ᵀᴴ 1940

Although the shipyard was very busy with people coming and going with tools, materials, and paint pots, Pearson was able to find a quiet corner behind some large wooden crates. There he rummaged through the haversack. There were some sandwiches and a slice of home-made cake as well as a bottle of cold tea. There was no money, but there were some letters. After he had finished eating the food, he took one out of its envelope and started to read it.

> *Dearest Clare,*
> *I'm not allowed to tell you where I am, but I can say that things are really hotting up here. We are in good spirits and life in the army isn't as bad as they say.*
> *I miss you so very much and I am longing for my first leave. I am sorry that you are having to work nights to make ends meet. I can understand that things must be very tough, but try to keep your lovely smile.*
> *Give my love to your mum and thank her for looking after little Jenny while you work...*

He put the letter back into the envelope. He could not read more. Strangely, for him, he suddenly had a feeling of guilt. Whether it was for eating this poor lady's food or reading a letter not intended for him to see, he would not have understood. Putting the letter back into the bag and rummaging further in it, he saw a photo. It was a picture of a man in army uniform.

Pearson put it back and fastened the haversack. Then, when he was sure that he was unobserved, he hung the bag where it would be seen, on a sign-post on the path leading to the river.

There was a security fence along the side of the wharf. He had noticed people showing what he thought was a pass at the guarded gate to gain access to their workplace on the minesweeper. He wandered along to the gate and stood behind the queue of workers waiting to enter. It was immediately obvious to him that he would not be able go through, so he wandered along the inside of the fence towards the stern of the warship. There was a commotion going on when he reached a point level with the *Bee*. Men were shouting and giving and acknowledging instructions. He could not stand there watching, drawing attention to himself, so Pearson walked someway past and found a gap between some more large packing cases where he could watch the large sheets of metal being lifted from the quay and lowered into the ship's hold. As he watched, he racked his brain about how he could get on the ship without being noticed and if he did, where would he find refuge?

At length, the last of the load was lowered on to the ship. Could he hide in the hold? He wondered. This thought was quickly abandoned when he saw three of the crew start to place heavy planks across the wide space. When that was done, they unrolled a large tarpaulin and spread it over the planks.

One of the three went round the deck checking that the cover was properly in place. When he was satisfied, he shouted, "Bert, get the fire stoked and put a kettle on!"

"Aye, Skipper," was the response.

"Alf, can you shorten the line on our pinnace and bring it round tight behind the stern and the wharf to stop it banging on the hull during the night."

"Aye, Ben. Don't want to lose sleep tonight with a dinghy thumpin' against the ship with the wash from every passing craft. We got to be up before dawn."

"What time is dawn, Ted?"

"About four, but I gotta be up before, to get the engines goin'," answered Ted.

Pearson could not see the dinghy being moved, only the figure of Alf as he dragged the smaller craft's towing line up against the quay.

"Bugger me," whispered Pearson to himself. "That's it, if I can't get on the ship, I will now be able reach to get on to the dinghy. And where the ship goes, that boat will be towed too!"

He was re-invigorated by thought of his idea. But then, he remembered – he still had to get through the security fence to access the quay. His joy was cruelly tempered.

As dusk began to fall, he was feeling desperate and decided to take a chance. Thinking aloud, he whispered, "This fence must end somewhere. I wonder if I can get round the end of it?"

He stood up and cautiously looked left and right to see if there was anyone on the pathway parallel with the quay. The workers were all on the warship, out of sight. He understood that if they were working through the night, they would need electric light. The blackout would mean that they could not illuminate outside work, and they were working inside. The place was deserted!

Pearson strolled along the side of the fence, away from the ships. Eventually, he reached the end of the path.

"Bloody hell, barbed wire," he said looking at the very end of the fence. However, he felt a sudden thrill when he saw, in the failing light, that there was a gate in the fence. He gave it a push. There was a clank of chain pulling against a padlock. The gate was locked.

Pearson took the padlock in his hand and, in the failing light tried to see what kind it was. He recognised the make and, holding it with one hand, he searched in his overall pocket for the skeleton key he had used much earlier in the day. Thankfully, he had not dropped it when he rushed off with bike. A short while later, he had the lock in one hand and the removed chain in the other.

• • • • • • • • • ● • • • • • • • • • •

The boiler suit, which by now was perfectly dry, offered poor protection from the cold of the night in the damp dinghy. Pearson had crept up under the thwart that the oarsman would normally sit on, but it was the only protection he had. His fitful sleep was brought to an abrupt end by the shocking sound of an alarm ringing inside the hull of the ship. The stowaway was instantly alert. The noise stopped. There was silence apart from the slop of the wavelets gently rocking the pinnace. Pearson crept further under the thwart to hide as best he could. Then there was the clang of metal against metal and the slam of a door. Some seagulls angrily protested about the early morning disturbance. A grating sound was obviously someone clearing his throat. It was followed by the hiss of air being released as he spat. Some moments of silence were interrupted before a continuous gurgle of water hitting water near to the dinghy.

"He's having a piss over the side of the ship," Pearson said to himself.

Then, all silent again for a few seconds before the clang of metal against metal and the slamming of a door. Pearson was now wide awake. Sheltered by the hull of the ship, he could not see sky beginning to brighten in the east, but from what he had heard last night, he realised that it must soon be dawn. And then it would be light, and he might be spotted by a member of the crew. He began to get very nervous as he lay contorted in the bottom of the boat.

A clang from inside the hull of the ship, very near to him. Then another. A whirring sound. Two loud bangs accompanied black smoke spewing out of a pipe in the stern on the side where he was. Then it stopped and he could see black smudges of exhaust smoke as it rose into the sky and caught the first rays of the sun. The performance was repeated, but this time, the whirring did not stop, and neither did the sooty smoke, which was now being propelled out of the pipe. The engine was running!

An unseen hand did something in the engine room. The sound and smoke decreased in volume. Instead of the previous frantic pace, there was now a rhythmical, steady "pom, pom, pom", and with each "pom", a puff of grey smoke and a jet of water was expelled from the pipe.

Pearson paid no attention to the same performance being enacted on the starboard side as the second engine was started up. He had been distracted by a shout.

"Alf, change the stern line to a slip and come back on board."

"Aye, Ben," answered the man.

Pearson was terrified, for the man was climbing ashore almost above his head. "He's bound to see me," the boy said to himself.

Alf climbed back onto the ship, oblivious of the ship pinnace's occupant.

"Let go the bow line, Bert!" shouted a voice. That must be the captain giving orders, thought the boy.

There was the sound of a bell ringing and the pace of the engine quickened.

"Slip the stern, Alf!"

Pearson could hear the noise of a heavy rope landing on the deck as the shore line was pulled on board. Suddenly the dinghy was forcibly jerked forward as the line between it and the ship tightened and the tow began. Pearson puffed a great sigh of relief. He was off to sea!

Out of the shadow of the *Bee* now, and bathed in the early morning sunshine, Pearson could see the huge grey hull of the warship as they passed it. He was elated at his achievement. He had escaped and was on his way to freedom!

As they left the shelter of the harbour, the small boat began writhing, twisting, and bucking in the swell. Pearson freed himself from his position under the thwart and sat up on the floor of the boat. The degree of movement of his vessel was beginning to worry him. It did not feel safe. Now too, the exhaust was unpleasantly noxious and the hot water spouting out of the pipe was drenching him. His so-recent elation was quickly turning to terror. He held tightly to the thwart, and as the ship got further from the shore he became increasingly uncomfortable about his new environment. It was much colder outside of the shelter of the harbour. How long would this journey take! Soon, his anxiety and discomfort increased to an unbearable level. He had to do something!

"Captain, Captain! Help, help!" he called. He kept repeating this at the top of his voice.

But there was no help for him. Ted, the engineer who was nearest to the stern, was in the engine room enjoying the bacon sandwich and tea Bert had delivered to him just before they left Cowes. The noise of the two mighty Bolinder engines completely drowned out any other sounds. Likewise, Ben was busy. In the wheelhouse, he had his sandwich in one hand and steered with the other. He was deep in thought as he gripped the wheel. He was used to skippering the *Bee*, but two new complications had made it more difficult. First, the Solent was being increasingly visited by enemy aircraft. So far there had been no bombing, but a slow-moving craft such as this was an easy target. Second, since last year, the BBC had been banned from broadcasting weather forecasts as it was feared that they gave the enemy strategic information. So, for two reasons, ships' captains had to keep a careful eye on the sky. Ben was mentally engaged in considering the factors that would determine their arrival time in Portsmouth. He had already noticed the gathering dark thunder clouds to the south-east, the direction the wind was coming from. The sea route from Cowes to Portsmouth was ten nautical miles. With their heavy load, the *Bee* could make around six knots. It would be low tide in two hours, so with some tide against them, the voyage would take at least another hour. There was a risk of them getting very wet and being buffeted by a squall before they made port.

Alf and Bert were in the crew's quarters at the bow of the vessel enjoying the warmth of the coke stove as they also breakfasted. They had closed the hatch door to keep in the heat.

And so, Pearson's calls for help went unanswered. He had to continue to endure the misery and discomfort he was completely unable to escape from. Unknown to him, if the captain was right about the risk of foul weather, the boy's situation would soon get even worse.

"Another cuppa, Skipper?"

Bert had walked along the deck to the wheelhouse carrying the teapot in a basket.

"Just the job, lad. Don't feel like early summer, do it?

Bert poured some tea and, using a spoon, scooped some artificial milk out of a tin and plunged it into the tea mug.

"Another spoon of Fussles, if you please. It's going to be a very long day."

Fussles was the legendary tinned sweet milk widely used on ships, where it was impossible to keep milk fresh.

As Bert was making to leave, Ben said, "I forgot to mention it, but can you check that Alf let out the long line on the tow of the dinghy. Otherwise, it'll be gettin' sodden wet from the exhaust."

Bert put the basket down on the wheelhouse floor, opened the door, and disappeared in the direction of the stern. He was not long gone when the door was wrenched open. Bert stood wide mouthed in the opening, facing the skipper.

"You ain't gonna believe this, Skipper!"

"What, what is it!"

"There's a bloke on the pinnace. He be sittin' on the floor!"

"You must be joking! Here, take the wheel, keep her on this course and look out sharp for mines."

Ben waited for Bert to take over and then hastily left.

Chapter 5

WEDNESDAY MORNING, 29TH MAY 1940

Ben was a very level-headed person; in fact his unexcitable nature caused some to find him quite boring. Thus it was, that as he stood with hands on the stern rail, he took some time to deliberate about what should be done. Clearly, this lad was desperate to leave the island, but why? No matter. At issue was his responsibility for his ship and the crew. If they turned round and took the miscreant back to Cowes, delivery of the urgent cargo would be delayed, and they would not get away from Portsmouth in time to catch the high tide needed to sail from Cowes to Newport on their return. This would lead them to spend another night away from home.

"Please, Captain, please can I come on to the ship. I'm very cold. Please!"

Ben said nothing. He had made his decision. He turned round, twisted the handle on the engine hatch door, and swung it open. There was the clang of metal on metal that Pearson heard the night before, as the door struck a railing.

The captain used the full strength of his voice, "Ted, put engines out of gear. We need to stop the ship,"

The engineer was already alerted to the fact that something untoward had happened when the door opened. He knew Ben well enough to realise that it was something urgent, and without question he swung two levers to an upright position.

Looking up at Ben, he shouted, "What's up?"

"Come up and give me a hand, we got a passenger."

Ted wiped his greasy hands on a cloth and then climbed up the companion way to the deck.

Alf had noticed the change in the rhythm of the engine. As his head popped up from the door to the crew's quarters, he immediately saw that Bert was steering the ship. Where was the captain? He hurried along the deck and found Ted and Ben busy loosening the line to the dinghy. A few steps more and he saw the whole surprising scenario.

"Alf, pull the dinghy alongside on the windward side, so we don't lose it. The deck's too high here to get the boy on board."

A few minutes later, with the joint effort of Ben and Alf, Pearson was dragged onto the deck.

"Who the hell are you?" asked Alf with a threatening tone.

"We'll find out soon enough. Get him below, give him a blanket, and dry off his overalls by the stove."

Alf scowled at the youth as he said, "Come on, follow me."

Very unsteadily, grasping at the rail as he walked, Pearson followed the ship hand.

"Ted, rather than mess up our schedule, we'll take the lad to Portsmouth and hand him over to the police there. I reckon he's run off from somewhere."

"Can't be Parkhurst Prison, he's too young."

"Aye, he is. Let's get goin' again."

Just over an hour later, Ben saw the hatch to the crew's quarters open and the two deckhands emerge. They had been sheltering from the rain and the tell-tale smoke from the thin metal chimney showed that they had been doing so in some comfort. They both made their way to the wheelhouse and Bert opened the door.

"Well, what do you make of the lad?" asked the captain.

"He's dead to the world, snorin' like a baby, but not before he ate two bacon sandwiches," answered Alf.

"Did you find out anything about him?"

"No, Ben, he just said that he was runnin' away. But what was strange was that when we got his overalls off him to dry them, underneath he had a white vest and black sports shorts on."

"And he was wearing black plimsoles, like you use for PE," interrupted Bert.

"Get ready for berthin', we just got the "permission to enter" flag from the harbour master," announced Ben, who had been watching and waiting for the signal flag to be raised on a mast mounted on the stone wall ahead of them. This gave the *Bee* priority over other shipping, to enter the harbour and dock at the quay near to the metal works where their cargo was to be unloaded.

"What shall we do with the boy?"

"When we berth, wake him up and give him a cup of tea and something to eat. Tell him to stay down there until we have unloaded. Best lock the hatch so he can't do a runner before the police take care of him. We don't want no fuss from him, we got to unload quickly so that we can turn round and sail for home, the weather don't look good. It'll take us three or four hours at least till we have an empty hold."

Twenty minutes later, the *Bee* was safely moored by the quayside and Ted had cut the engines. The vessel was expected. A tractor towing a large trailer pulled up alongside the ship and two dock workers appeared from a shed to help with the unloading.

"Ted, can you look after the crane while I goes to find a policeman?"

"What, for the lad?"

"Yeah, I don't have in mind to take him back with us. I got enough worry with a crew to care for, I don't want to have the nipper as well. Besides, he might be a criminal."

"Yes, I suppose you're right."

Ben clambered ashore and after exchanging some words with the two men, he walked off in the direction they were pointing.

Ted was operating the derrick, the ship's crane, when the captain reappeared. He was alone. Ben waited for a steel sheet to be swung past him, and onto the trailer, before he climbed back aboard. He walked to the mast and shouted over the noise of the crane engine, "That was a waste of time! This is a naval base of course, the only police inside the walls are military ones. They just laughed when I explained the situation. Anyways, they said they would telephone the local coppers and ask them to collect the lad from the ship."

"Looks like someone has followed you, Ben."

The captain turned round to look in the direction Ted was pointing. On the other side of the trailer, hurrying towards the ship, was a young man carrying a briefcase and looking very distinguished in a smart naval officer's uniform.

He too had to wait for a sheet to be swung past him before he could continue walking. He looked very much out of place among the men working on the quay. His navy-blue jacket with rank insignia on the shoulders and sleeves, his white shirt and black tie, and his peaked white cap contrasted with the slovenly appearance of those handling the steel sheets. To Ben's astonishment the naval officer started to climb aboard.

"You must have upset them, Ben, that's a sub-lieutenant, see the gold flash on his sleeve."

"I thought that you were in the army, Ted."

"Oh, I've had a few dealings with navy officers on troop transports," whispered Ted.

The two men watched as the officer spoke to Bert, who was standing by the side of the hold, nearest to the shore. He pointed at Ben. The officer walked round the hold towards the mast. Ted slowed the engine to its quietest level.

"Captain Bainbridge?"

"The same. To what do we owe the honour of a visit from the navy?" answered Ben.

"I am Sub-Lieutenant Russell," said the man, offering his hand. "I would like to speak with you privately."

Ben shook hands and then lifted his flat cap, scratched his head and said, "Best we go to the wheelhouse. Ted, can you keep the unloadin' going."

"Aye, Skipper."

The two men walked round the hold and up the step through the open door of the wheelhouse.

"Well, how can I help you, Sub-Lieutenant?"

"I have an urgent message for you from the Admiralty. I am ordered to commandeer this vessel, immediately, for use by the navy and to take command of it."

He opened his briefcase and took out an unsealed brown envelope. Pushing it towards Ben, he said, "You will find written confirmation of the order in this envelope."

Ben took it but did not bother to read the contents. He lifted his cap again and exhaled loudly.

"What? You want to take the *Bee*? What's goin' to happen to the crew?"

"They will have to find their own way home. However, I am instructed to say that it would be of great value to the navy and to the war effort if you and any of your crew would agree to serve on the vessel. It is appreciated that you have vast experience of voyaging in this craft and the mission we are to undertake requires good seamanship."

"Where'd we being going, then?"

"I can't tell you that yet, but I must warn you that it will involve great danger."

After a pause, while Ben briefly considered the man's words, he said, "Well, let's ask the men then."

"Yes, of course. Can you stop the loading so that I can address them?"

"Yes, we can finish it later. Let me give the order."

They left the wheelhouse and walked round to the mast. By this time the word had gone round the ship, and the shore workers, that something unusual was going on.

"Ted, can you stop the crane engine and hang on here a bit? The officer wants to talk to us."

When the motor noise stopped, Ben called out to his deckhands, "Alf, Bert, come on over here, Sub-Lieutenant Russell wants to talk to us all."

In a few moments, all the crew were gathered by the mast, eager to hear what their visitor had to say. It was a motley gathering. Four men in open neck shirts, various forms of working clothes ranging from worn jackets, a waistcoat, and blue engineers' overalls. Each of the men had a flat cap, most of them very well used. And on one side stood the officer wearing a uniform that was so clean and fresh that it could have been new.

"Men, the British troops fighting in Europe are facing tough resistance from the Germans. So tough in fact, that they have had to retreat. This is partly because the Belgians have surrendered." His voice was very clipped and formal. A voice used to giving orders to lower ranks. He pulled a newspaper out of his briefcase and waved it in the air. There was disdain in his voice as he said, "I have with me a copy of yesterday's *Evening News* for you to read. You'll see that King Leopold of Belgium ordered the capitulation of the army, against the will of his government. His tone changed as he continued, "In the same paper you can also see that the British forces in Boulogne, on the French coast, have been evacuated by the navy."

There were comments among those listening, but the officer continued.

"The Admiralty has been asked to support a large, combined-forces operation, which was launched at zero, eight, five, seven on Sunday 26th May. To this end, I have with me an order to commandeer the *Motor Vessel Bee* and to put the ship at the disposal of the navy. This is with immediate effect."

"What we goin' do then?" blurted Bert.

The officer was clearly not going to tolerate interruptions and said, curtly, "Please keep questions until I have finished."

He paused a moment and then continued.

"As merchant marine sailors, the navy cannot give you orders. You are all permitted to leave the ship when you have discharged your cargo, and a naval crew will be put aboard. However, the navy recognises that you have vast experience of handling this vessel and it would be appreciated if any of you would agree to stay aboard."

This time, Ted made the mistake of commenting.

"What good is an unarmed motor barge to the navy?"

Sub-Lieutenant Russell was clearly used to his rank being respected. He said abruptly, "As I said, please wait until I have finished." There was a short, resentful silence before he continued.

"In short, I am asking if any of you would volunteer to man the *Bee* in what will be a very dangerous operation. I can give no guarantee of you returning safely. I can give you no further information about the intended role of the ship apart from the fact that it will sail today.

"I will give you five minutes to decide your choice: stay aboard or catch the ferry back to the Isle of Wight."

The officer turned to the man in the blue boiler suit and said, "I take it that you are the engineer. I would like to look at the engine room while you are making your decisions."

Ted pointed towards the stern and said, "Help yourself."

When the lieutenant was out of earshot, Ben used his authority to direct the conversation.

"Well, what do you blokes think? For my part, I missed action in that last war, now seems to be my chance."

Ted, as second in command of the vessel, commented next.

"Well, you've all heard my stories of the last show, I'd be happy to serve king and country again. Besides, I can guarantee that there ain't an engineer in the King's navy as could start a Bollinder engine, let alone keep it goin.'" "What about you, Alf?" asked Ben.

"I don't think I could look my kids in the eye and say that I never did my bit to beat the Jerries."

Ben slapped him on the back and joked, "You might get a medal to show 'em."

He turned to the youngest of the crew and said, "Bert, you's just eighteen and have got a long life ahead of you. We other blokes are well on in years and have probably had our best ones already. I'm certain that we'd all advise you to skip ship and go home."

There were noises of agreement from the other two crew, but they were counteracted by Bert's shaking of his head.

"No, no I ain't going to sit at home wondering what you blokes are about and even worse to meet you when you get back and hear of your adventure. No, Skipper, I'm coming too!"

"Think about it, Bert, maybe we won't come back," said Ted.

"That's a risk I'll take, just like you blokes are," the young man said in a determined voice.

The conversation abruptly ended when Ted said, "'Ere he comes, wonder what he made of the engines."

They all turned to see the officer making his way around the hold to join them.

"Well, men, are any of you willing to stay on board?" he asked crisply.

The crew looked at their captain to respond.

"You got yourself a crew here, them navy lads will have to find passage on another craft!"

The lieutenant's face beamed. "Splendid, that's very good news. Let me just clarify the situation. I am to be in command of the ship, and I rely on Captain Bainbridge and you crew to get it safely to where it is needed and operate it there. Is that acceptable to all?"

There was a chorus of assent.

"As this is now a ship of the British navy, you must address me as Lieutenant. As befits his status, I will address Captain Bainbridge as "Captain". However, unless you object, the rest of you I will address by first names. No saluting necessary. Everyone happy with that?"

Once again there were sounds of agreement from Alf and Bert but not from Ted.

"So, let's get the cargo off and make ready for sea. I must go ashore to make some arrangements, requisition provisions, and obtain equipment. Ted, how much fuel have you got?"

"We bunkered in Newport, so we should have enough for around forty hours at full speed."

"Good. And water, Captain?"

"There's a fresh-water tank on the starboard side by the wheelhouse. About half full I expect."

"Have a hose got to the tap on the quayside and fill it."

"Aye, aye. Bert, can you see to that while the rest of us finish unloading?"

"Aye, Skipper."

"Captain, I need to get some information from you. Can we go to the wheelhouse?"

The two men walked to the simple wooden structure where Ben spent most of his time. Once inside, the sub-lieutenant surveyed the interior. The only furniture was a tall stool that allowed the helmsman to sit when on a longer passage. The equipment consisted of the binnacle, a wooden post with a large compass across the top at about waist height; a lever telegraph that relayed instructions to the engineer; and a voice tube through which the helmsman could speak to the engine room. The once white-painted walls were stained to a shade of light brown, the result of Ben's frequent pipe smoking. In front of the wooden spoked wheel that steered the ship, at the bottom of the windows, there was a broad shelf for the logbook and other documents.

Opening his briefcase, the lieutenant took out a notebook and pencil. "Captain, in all haste, I have to make sure that your vessel has what is necessary to make a sea voyage, which may take over twelve hours."

"Can you tell me where to?"

"Not until we leave port, but I can tell you that we will be sailing east."

Ben was quiet while he quickly considered what difficulties might arise.

"Does that worry you?"

"Not overly, Lieutenant, but it would be very helpful to have a weather forecast."

"Yes, I assumed that you would say that. I will get tide times and weather forecasts for you."

"As regards weather, Lieutenant, you must understand that this ship has a flat bottom. It is designed to be able to take to the ground at low tide in the ports we visit. The downside of such a hull is that the ship will roll heavily in a strong side wind. It will be much worse for us today as the ship will have no cargo to act as ballast. This might affect the speed we can travel."

"I understand. What is the ship's maximum speed?"

"In still water, she'll do eight knots with a light cargo. Generally, we make an average of seven knots."

"Good, that's a reasonable speed. Now, we need to communicate with other ships and possibly the shore. Do you have any signal flags or a signal lamp?"

"No, nothin' like that on board."

"What about sea charts?"

"Same with that, the routes we usually take, I know like the back of my hand."

"What about first aid equipment?"

"Yes, we have a small first aid box in the crew quarters."

"A hand compass?"

"No, the only compass is the one in front of you on the binnacle."

"Firefighting equipment?"

"Only the bare necessity – a hose and fire extinguishers."

"How about provisions?"

"We clubbed together and used our meat ration coupons to have a bacon fry-up last night. We hadn't expected to have to have a meal on board this evening. We got some tins of corned beef, beans, sweetened milk, and so on, but that's all."

"Right, I have listed what we need. As regards rationed food goods, this won't be a problem for men on active service. I will need a couple of hours to source these things. I'll arrange for them to be brought alongside in a truck for loading on board."

He looked at his watch and said, "It is 16.00 hours. High water is at 16.34, so we will be leaving on the ebb tide. Prepare to slip our berth at 19.00. Oh, by the way, how much water does the *Bee* draw?"

"Loaded, she needs a fathom of water, about six feet."

"Fine. That long ladder lying on the quay, does that belong to the ship?"

"Yes, we'll take it on board when we have unloaded."

"Do you really need it? It must clutter the decks. I want them clear."

"We have it in case we have to go over the side at low tide to clear any rubbish on the propellers. At sea we stow it up against the mast, out of the way."

The officer thought for a moment and then said, "Oh, all right, perhaps we should take it.

I'll see you in about two hours."

He put his notebook away and left. Ben watched as he circuited round the pile of steel sheets before he hurried towards one of the high red brick buildings in the dockyard.

An hour later, the last of the metal sheets had been unloaded and the tractor and trailer had left.

"Right, Alf and Bert, get most of the hold covered so's we're ready to go as soon as we gets the provisions on board. Better leave a bit open in case we gotta stow some provisions and equipment in there. Get the ladder stowed as usual. When you done that, stoke up the stove and let's have a brew up. We'll eat later when the navy rations get here."

"Aye, Captain. Do you want me to put a slip on the mooring lines so's we can cast off quickish later?" asked Alf.

"Good idea. Bert, can you bring mine and Ted's tea to the stern, I need to have a chat with him."

"Aye, Captain."

Later, Ben joined Ted in the engine room and took the tea mugs from Bert when he passed them down. There was only one stool in the small space, so Ben took it and Ted, his overalls already besmirched with oil, sat on an oil drum.

"Well, Ted, this is a turn up ain't it?"

"You can say that again. Where do you think we're goin'?"

"I was about to ask you, with your military experience, the same thing"

"Well, I thought first that they wanted us to transport equipment somewhere. That's the obvious thing for a cargo ship to do ain't it?"

"Yeah, you'd think so, but he made it clear that it's only supplies that we'll be loading."

"He never told you anything, then?"

"No, but he did say that we will be going east."

"There's only one country that way. I haven't been there since 1918, and I certainly didn't think I would ever see it again."

"What, France you mean?"

"Yeah. Now that I think about, he mentioned that the army had been evacuated from Boulogne. I wonder if they want us to freight some of their equipment back to England?"

"Now, that must be it!"

"Perhaps he'll tell us more this evening."

"Ted, the reason I wanted a chat was that he told me that our voyage might take more than twelve hours. Once we're at sea, through the night, there ain't much for the lads to do, whereas you got to work flat out to keep the engines goin'. I know how tricky them engines are. I was goin' to ask if you would like to have Bert here to give you a hand so's you can get some rest."

"Kind of you to ask, Skipper, but I think I can manage. I'll keep it in mind."

Ben got up to go but then hesitated.

"Um, Ted, do you think that this young naval feller knows what he's doing?"

"Why do you ask?"

"I got a feelin' that he underestimates the difficulties of night sailin' along the coast. Bear in mind, Ted, there are no shore lights, 'cause of the blackout and only very few light houses are allowed to be working. Them as are can only come on for four minutes on the hour."

"Yeah, I been wonderin' about that too. And we won't be alone out there, could be some big navy ships, but we won't see no one with the wartime ban on navigation lights. But Ben, I do know that to be a sub-lieutenant he must be pretty good. He has to have studied at Dartmouth College for at least three years before he can be a midshipman, and at least two more before he makes his present rank."

"Still, I reckon night navigation is goin' to be tricky."

"You'll have to nursemaid him, Ben."

Ben paused, lifted his cap, scratched his head, and then replied, "I will that."

The skipper paused again and then said, "Ted, I couldn't but notice that you weren't too happy about him callin' crew by first names."

"Ah, it don't matter, Ben, it was just an issue of pride, I suppose. As you know, in the Great War, in Flanders, I was promoted, in the field, from sergeant to sub-lieutenant."

"Oh, I see what you mean, so he should be callin' you 'lieutenant', not 'Ted'."

"Happens he should. But I ain't going to make a fuss about. That is, unless he riles me!"

"He'd better make sure he don't come into the engine room without your permission then!"

The two men laughed, and Ben took the remains of his now cold tea to the wheelhouse to enjoy it with a pipe of tobacco.

Chapter 6

WEDNESDAY 29ᵀᴴ MAY 1940, 18.05

It was just after six o'clock that an open back military lorry pulled up alongside the *Bee*. Two naval ratings got out of the cab. One of them started to pull down the tailgate while the other strode to the side of the boat and, in the direction of the wheelhouse, called out, "Skipper, got a delivery for you."

Ben knocked the tobacco out of his pipe and stamped on the sparks that had fallen to the deck.

"Do we need to use the derrick?"

"No, the crew should be able to manage the stuff."

By this time Alf and Bert were walking along the narrow deck towards where Ben stood.

"Go ashore and help the sailors get the goods on board."

The men nodded, climbed onto the quay, and went to the back of the lorry.

Ted now stood behind Ben. He whispered, "Why do they need a lorry? We only need provisions.""Well, there's something heavy they're pulling out."

There was a dull thud as a huge bundle of rope thumped down on to the ground behind the lorry. The men started to drag it to the ship. When they reached the edge of the quay, it was obvious that Ted and Ben would have to help lift the load.

"Hang on, we'll have to put it into the hold, I'll open it up a bit more!" shouted Ben.

As he struggled to uncover more of the canvas and lift the planks under it, he suddenly saw a pair of arms, clothed in blue overalls, reach past him to help drag the cover off.

Ben glanced round and saw Pearson standing beside him.

"Stone me, lad, I'd forgotten about you. Here, help me lift this plank."

The seven of them hauled and pushed the bundle onto the deck and then heaved it up and let it fall into the hold.

Ben asked the sailors what the others in the crew had been thinking. "What in God's name do we need that for?"

"Don't ask me, Skipper, I just takes orders and don't ask questions. We were just told to load up provisions, some other gear, and these scramblin' nets."

"Why would we need scrambling nets?" asked Alf.

"No doubt you'll get orders in due course to tell you."

Rain had started to fall, and Ben stopped the speculation among the crew, saying, "Let's get the other stuff on board. Form a chain and pass the stuff on."

Ben stood back and watched as a number of cardboard boxes were lifted from the lorry and passed on to the ship.

"Take the ones labelled provisions down to the crew's quarters at the bow," he instructed.

"What about this one!?" shouted Alf from the quayside.

"What's the label say?"

"Says 'first aid', Skipper." "Put that by the wheelhouse, I'd better keep it there."

"And this one? It says, 'Caution: Fragile Equipment, Handle With Care.'" "Same thing, by the wheelhouse."

"Captain, careful with that, our lives may depend on it!" shouted a voice from the direction of the bow. Ben leant forward and saw the dark blue rain-coated figure of the sub-lieutenant hurrying along the cobbled quay, carrying a large duffel bag of the same colour over his shoulder.

The officer climbed aboard and immediately made his way to the wheelhouse. As he passed Ben he said, "Captain, we need a briefing, if you please."

Ben called to the crew, "Get the hold covered and get into the dry. Alf, check the provisions to see what we've got and get some supper made. You'd better take the boy down with you out of the rain until the police get here to pick him up."

The captain waited while the officer shook out his raincoat through the open door and then joined him inside.

"Captain, I want preparations made to leave as soon as possible. We have official clearance to pass through the harbour entrance at 19.30."

"Just a moment, I must tell the lieutenant to get the engines warmed."

"Who?"

"Ted, the engineer, he had the rank of sub-lieutenant in the army before he started on the boats."

There was a pause.

"Oh, I see. Thanks for telling me."

Ben leant over the voice tube by the wooden back wall and shouted, "Ted, do you hear me?"

The two men waited for a moment, and then there was the sound of a muffled voice. "Aye, Skipper. I hear you."

"We leave in forty-five minutes, at 19.30. Have the engines ready, please."

"Aye, aye."

Ben stood up and looked at the officer.

"I trust you have some information for me."

"Indeed, I have permission to tell you where you are going. Our destination is Ramsgate. Have you been there before?"

If Ben was shocked, he didn't show it and just said, "Um...I have that, though not as skipper."

"Was it on this ship?"

"The very same, though in the opposite direction. In 1928, the original ship, called the *Bee*, a gaff sailer with no engine, which I had sailed on since I was fourteen years old, was replaced by this ship. I was in the crew that went to Faversham, where she was built, to pick her up and take her back to Newport. We stopped overnight at Ramsgate."

"Quite a story. You must tell me about the sailing ship when we have more time. In Ramsgate, we will pick up orders from the Admiralty."

"From what you indicate, you are in a hurry to get there."

"It is of the utmost urgency that we proceed with all available speed, by the shortest possible course. Not only are we in a hurry, but the area through which we travel is also a favourite hunting ground for U-boats and fast surface attackers, the E-boats. The speedier we travel, the lower the risk."

"Well, as I said earlier, our top speed is eight knots, but a voyage that long at top speed would put more strain than I like to think on the engines, so I would advise at best we try for seven knots. Do you know the distance in sea miles?"

"A hundred and twenty nautical miles by the most direct route."

Ben tried to calculate the time the voyage might take, but the officer was there before him.

"About seventeen hours."

"So, allowing for adverse winds and foul tides, perhaps twenty hours, then. What about the weather, did you get a forecast?"

The man reached into the briefcase he had put on the floor and took out some documents. He picked one of them and showed it to Ben.

"This is an admiralty forecast. Be mindful that it is confidential. However, it is a bit too general for our needs."

Districts.	FORECASTS FOR THE 24 HOURS COMMENCING 12 NOON, G.M.T. 28th May, 1940.
1 S.E. England 2 E. England 3 E. Midlands 4 W. Midlands	Light or moderate southeast wind, veering southwest; thundery rain with local thunderstorms at first; bright periods and showers later; average temperature.
5 S.W. England 6 South Wales	Moderate southwest wind; bright intervals, showers, local thunder; average temperature.
7 North Wales 8 N.W. England 9 N. Midlands 10 N.E. England 11 S.E. Scotland 12 S.W. Scotland & Isle of Man.	Light or moderate south to southeast wind, veering southwest later; thundery rain with local thunder; bright intervals tomorrow morning; average temperature.
13 { A. W. Scotland B.N.W. Scotland 14 Mid Scotland 15 N.E. Scotland 16 Orkneys and Shetlands	Light or moderate southeast wind, veering south to southwest later; bright intervals and local showers at first; occasional rain later; local coast fog; local thunder; average temperature.
17 N.W. Ireland 18 N.E. Ireland 19 S.E. Ireland 20 S.W. Ireland	Light variable wind, finally southwest, moderate; bright intervals, showers; local thunderstorms; average temperature.

Ben took his cap off and scratched his head as he read the page. Then he commented, "So the south-east wind will slow us down until it veers to south-west."

"I've also got a more recent Met Office forecast from 18.00 this evening."

He sorted through the documents, picked out one, and then read it out.

"Wind south, south-west, force four. Visibility good. Sea state two on a scale of zero to nine."

"That sounds better, but she will roll some with force four."

"So be it, Captain. Any other worries?"

"Yes, Selsey Bill."

"Wait a minute, I have Admiralty charts covering our voyage."

The officer took several folded documents from his briefcase. He flicked through the labels on the charts and chose one.

"This chart covers Portsmouth almost to Eastbourne. Help me hold it up."

The two men took a corner each and held the large chart up, for it was much too big to put on the window ledge. With his free hand,

Ben pointed to a feature on the map that showed where land jutted out into the sea in a *v* shape.

He said, "That's Selsey Bill. The sea is shallow around there, but there is a narrow channel called the Looe Channel, which, as I remember it, is marked by port and starboard buoys. In daylight, in good weather, 'tis no problem to find. The alternative to going through this narrow waterway is to take a very wide circle in deep water round all the shallows. This takes a vessel right out into the English Channel and lengthens the voyage significantly."

"And raises the risk of being found by the enemy," interrupted the officer. "So, we take the Looe Channel, then."

"And that's what causes me concern."

"Why?"

"Well, I checked in my almanac."

"Checked what?"

"Sunset! Today, the sunset is 20.55. Question is, can we get there before it's too dark to see the buoys, 'cause if we goes the wrong side of 'em we'll be wrecked."

Sub-Lieutenant Russell had significant experience of navigation, but the warships he had sailed in were of a size where they did not, and indeed could not, hug the coast in the fashion that the planned course of the *Bee* would.

"The buoys have no light signals?"

"Not in wartime, 'taint permitted now is it?"

"How far is it from Portsmouth to Selsey? Fold up the chart so that we just see the area we are interested in."

With some difficulty, Ben folded up the large chart to reveal their proposed course. Meanwhile, Sub-Lieutenant Russell foraged in his briefcase for something. He brought out a pair of dividers.

No words were exchanged as the officer used the implement to measure the distance.

Then he spoke. "Fourteen nautical miles. At full speed, it will take us just about two hours to reach the channel."

"So, if we get away at 19.30, we could make the position half an hour after sunset. Question is, will there be enough light for us to find them buoys. The weather won't help, it'll be a dark evenin' even if it don't rain. Don't forget, either, that the tide is on the ebb, it will slow us some."

"Well, I want to try. As you can see, once through that channel there is a long, straight safe passage with no shallows until we pass Eastbourne, and by that time it should be light. Did you check what time the dawn is?"

"Hang on, I wrote it on a paper by the wheel. Here we are, Wednesday 29th May, sunrise at 04.52, so the first light will be a fair bit before."

"After that, in daylight, navigation is going to be much easier. Anything else?"

"Can I tell the men about our destination?"

"Yes, but I suggest that we keep the question of passage through the Looe Channel just between us. There is no need to spread concern. Oh, just one delicate question from me."

"Go on."

"What are the toilet arrangements on the ship, is there a head?"

"Well things are simple on this ship. You pee over the lee side; if you chose the windward side you'll soon understand why t'other side is a better choice. As for other matters, there is a bucket on a rope round by the stern. We calls it, bucket and chuck it."

For the first time since they met, Ben saw the lieutenant smile.

"You need to get some bumf paper from Lieutenant Maynard. He keeps a supply of cut up newspaper."

Chapter 7

TWO HOURS EARLIER

Pearson had slept for most of the day, but in one break in his slumbers, he noticed that there were two of the crew's jackets hanging on one wall. He needed money for his escape! After listening a while to make sure that there was no one nearby on deck, he felt the inside pockets of the jackets. There was a wallet in one of them. He took it out and looked inside, There were two ten-shilling notes. He took them out and, although his overalls, hanging by the stove, were still damp, he put the money into one of the pockets.

He was dozing when he heard two of the crew open the hatch to their quarters. The light momentarily dazzled the youth as the men climbed down the companion way.

"Had a good rest then, lad, have you?" said Alf.

"Yeah, I was so bloody cold. It keeps warm down 'ere, dunnit?"

"Tis goin' to be warmer yet, we're having a brew up. Your overalls must be dry by now. Put them back, lad, there's a copper comin' to fetch you."

The dozy lad was suddenly galvanised.

"What, are they takin' me back to the island?"

"I should think so. Why? What did you have a mind to do?"

"Anythin' but to go back to the place I come from," he said as he put on his boiler suit while he thought of the thrashing he was due for.

"And where was that?" asked Bert.

"Don't matter. But I ain't going there. Can't I stay here?"

"As it happens, we ain't staying here for long. Pass me that coke bucket, Bert, will you?"

Alf put some coke on the embers and picked up a small bellows to blow air on the fire in the stove.

"But I could learn to work on the ship. I'm a good worker. I can cook, I swim better than any of my mates, and I'm good with my hands."

"Don't matter, mate, we got a full crew. Bert, take the bucket and get some fresh water from the tank."

Pearson watched as the younger member of the crew went up the steps. When he had gone, he said, "He ain't much older than me, what do I have to do to be a sailor?"

"Best thing you could do is to join the navy."

Pearson laughed and then blurted out, "Yeah, that would be good, but old man Baxter would only recommend me for the army."

"Who is 'old man Baxter'?"

"It don't matter. If you ain't goin'to help me, I'm going to scarper before the copper gets here."

Alf laughed as he said, "If you think you can escape from this place, you're going to be very disappointed. This is a Royal Navy harbour, it is surrounded by high walls with barbed wire on top, and the gates are manned by armed military police."

There was a long silence, punctuated only by the occasional oath from Pearson until the figure of Bert appeared at the top of the companionway.

"Go on, help him with the bucket, lad," said Alf. "Do something useful instead of just cussing your luck."

The resentful Pearson moved to the foot of the steps and lifted the bucket down.

"Everythin' all right, Bert?"

"Yeah, Skipper is with Ted in the engine room. They want me to take them their tea there."

Bert poured some water into the large metal kettle and put it on the now hot stove.

"I need a pee," said Pearson.

"Up you go, then, do it over the side. You want a cup of tea when you come back?"

"Yeah, thanks."

When Pearson emerged on deck, it was deserted. He looked around to see if what Alf had told him was true. Sure enough, there was a huge area surrounded by red brick walls. Men in blue uniforms were working in various places, loading big warships, tidying ropes, and hosing down the quayside, and lots of sailors were embarking up the gangways of some vessels, which were belching fumes from their funnels.

Down in the cabin, Bert said, "Did you find out who he is? When his clothes were dryin' and he was asleep, I saw he had some ugly scars on his back." "No, he ain't giving much away, but I have my suspicions. As I say, he's not very forthcoming." Alf paused and then said, "He could do with a lesson or two in manners and how to respect his elders and betters. Frankly, I don't think we'll see him again. He'll do a runner I expect, so don't bother pouring him any tea."

Just as Bert was about to take the two mugs of hot brew to the captain and Ted, there was a sound on the top companionway step. Black plimsolls and blue clad legs appeared as Pearson climbed down.

"Lesson one, lad, climb down companionway steps backwards, facing the steps. The way you are doin' it might seem quicker, but in any kind of heaving sea you could find yourself arrivin' down at the bottom faster than planned. Ain't that right, Bert?"

The other crew member winked and said, "It certainly is that."

"Well, do you believe now what I told you about trying to make a run for it here?" said Alf, smiling.

Pearson scowled. Giving an angry look at Alf, he blurted out, "You find that funny, do you? You bastard!"

Bert reacted and made move towards Pearson. Alf put his hand on his colleague's arm and said, "Let it be, Bert, we'll be rid of him soon."

Pearson seldom felt remorse, but now realised all too late, that he had ruined any chance he had of using these two to help him escape.

Nevertheless, he made a clumsy try at reconciliation when he said, "Sorry, Alf. I've had a hard time, and I ain't thinkin' right."

"Listen to me, lad. If you are ever to serve on a ship, big or small, respect for other crew members is all important. You live cheek by jowl in a cramped area and there just ain't no way you can do that peaceably without respect for others, especially them as has more experience or seniority."

"Yeah, I get that."

"And another thing. If you want to be respected yourself, always look for things that have to be done before you are ordered to do so. Just now you stood gawpin' while Bert was struggling with a heavy bucket. You should have jumped to help him without me tellin' you to."

"Yeah, yeah, I see what you mean."

"Right, havin' got that straight, how about a fag? How old are you anyway?

"Soon seventeen, why?"

"Then you are old enough to have a smoke."

Alf passed his packet of Wills Woodbines to Pearson. He took one and then passed it to Bert. Alf clicked his lighter, lit his cigarette and then passed the lighter to the others.

He took a long drawl, exhaled and then said, "Now, what about tellin' us who you are?"

The youth hesitated, but then thought, "What have I got to lose? These people can't help me."

"I'm Pearson. I escaped from St John's Approved School yesterday."

There was a long silence, eventually broken by Bert.

"Ain't you got another name?"

"Yeah, but I never use it."

"Why were you in the approved school?" asked Alf.

"Um, well several things really, I really got banged up 'cause I fell out with my mum's fancy man. That's to say I hit him, but I suppose the breakin' and entering charge didn't help."

This flow of information was fascinating the listeners. The older of them asked, "Where did you break in?"

"Well, you got to understand, this bloke, mum's fella, before she died, his name was Charlton, never bought anything for us. I forgot to say, I had a little brother. I was thirteen and he was seven. One day, through the window of a house in town, I saw some nice toys, just right for my brother."

Pearson stopped, suddenly mindful that he was talking too much.

"Well, what happened then?"

"Bert, the thing was, like it's difficult to explain, but the thing was the kid who lived in that house had loads of stuff, my brother had nothin', no toys or anything like that."

"So?"

"Well, I got into the house, only to find that there was a bloke inside. I give him a poke on the chin and scarpered."

"So, what happened?" asked Alf.

"Well, he run faster than me. He gave me a thump and dragged me to the cop shop."

The conversation continued until sometime later, when they heard the sound of a lorry very close to the ship and then the captain's unmistakable voice.

"Come on, Bert, we'd best be getting on deck. Pearson, you hang on in here until the copper comes."

Pearson did not answer. After the two had left, he put his hand into his pocket and took out the somewhat creased and damp ten-shilling notes. He straightened them out as best he could and restored them to the owner's wallet. He then climbed up two steps on the companionway and stood there to watch what was going on. He saw that all the crew and two sailors were struggling to get a large bundle on board. The captain was pulling the canvas cover off part of the hold. He was clearly having trouble lifting the planks underneath. Pearson hurried up the last two steps and along the deck to help him.

Chapter 8

WEDNESDAY 29ᵀᴴ MAY, 1940 - 9.25 HOURS

Sub-Lieutenant Russell was on his knees in the wheelhouse with the chart spread out on the floor. He had his dividers, a protractor, and a hand compass on the edge of the paper. In this position, he did not see Alf and Bert in deep conversation with Ben, by the mast. The "pomp", "pomp", "pomp" of the engines, ticking over in readiness, ensured that he could not hear their conversation either.

"What are we going to do with Pearson, Ben?"

"Could just stick him on the quayside to wait for the copper," said Bert.

"Can't leave him here in the rain, he ain't even got a coat," argued Alf.

"Did you never get wet? Let the kid experience a bit of discomfort."

"He got a bit of taste of that this morning, didn't he, Bert? So, what do you think, Ben?"

Despite the rain, the captain lifted his cap and scratched his head.

"Damned if I know what to do. Do he know anythin' useful?"

"He says he can cook and that he has trained in first aid. He says he wants to be an engineer," said Alf with a tone of desperation, which betrayed that he had some sympathy for Pearson's plight.

"Yeah, and he says he can swim well too!"

"I hopes that won't be necessary, Bert."

The tension was relieved as they all laughed.

"Do you know how old he is, Alf?"

"He says he's soon seventeen."

"Time he did a job of work then. Do he learn quick?"

"You have to on a ship, don't you, Skipper?"

"Right, unless the police show up in the next five minutes, we'll keep him on board. This evening we'll see how well he cooks. Alf, you show him the ropes, you've got a cabin boy with a lot to learn."

"He's got everything to learn."

"So, he's our fourth deckhand if you count Ted as such. It's going to be crowded in the crew's quarters, but there should be at least one person on deck all night to keep watch, so you will have to hot bed the bunks. The one comin' off watch take the bunk from the one goin' on. Alf, you work out a shift programme for the three of you. I'll break the news to Ted when I have the chance."

The door of the wheelhouse opened.

"Captain, we must go," called the officer.

"All ready to slip, Lieutenant," shouted Ben as he hurried back to the wheelhouse.

Very soon after he got there, he called out, "Bert, slip the bow." Ben watched as the bow was slowly blown off the quay by the south-westerly, now and then glancing astern to make sure there were no other ship movements. When he was convinced that there was no risk of the *Bee* swinging back in again, he pushed the telegraph lever to "Slow Ahead", and as soon as he heard the sound of the engine quicken, knowing that Ted had got the message, he shouted, "Slip stern, Alf!"

Ben glanced around the ship and, satisfied that all was well, he moved the lever to "Full Ahead". He knew that with the speed limit in the harbour at ten knots, he would not be in risk of going too fast and creating a wake that would annoy other mariners.

As they passed the Harbour Master's office, high up on the harbour wall, Ben opened the door of the wheelhouse and waved his cap in farewell to the men on watch.

"Take her towards the Horse Sands Fort and then turn to Nab Tower," said the lieutenant quietly.

"Aye, aye. Will you give me a course from the Nab, then?"

"Yes, Captain. What I want to do is to get as close as possible to the Tower and then give you a course directly to the Looe Channel. I have worked out the course on my chart."

"No shallows between the Nab and the channel?"

"No, none that you won't easily clear."

Ben turned the ship towards the massive stone fort that had stood guarding the entrance to Portsmouth Harbour since it was built seventy years earlier. At that time, it was to defend against an invasion by the French but now it had a new purpose, which was obvious from the anti-aircraft battery on the top. The other difference was that the once-grey, massive stone blocks used in its construction had been painted black and white in an attempt to camouflage it. Once they had left the building on their port side, the *Bee* turned east-south-east towards the strange construction five nautical sea miles away, where the lieutenant wanted a change of course.

"Captain, who is that young man in the boiler suit I saw looking at the fort just now?"

"Ah, yes, I'd been meaning to tell you. We have a stowaway on board."

The lieutenant was clearly irritated when he said, "A stowaway! How the hell did you miss seeing him?"

"Well, truth be told, I did see him. But couldn't do nothin' about it."

"What on earth do you mean?"

"He stowed away at Cowes. When I got to Pompey, I tried to get the police to fetch him, but they never come. So, we had to keep him."

"You should have told me; I could put him in the charge of the Military Police."

"I tried them, but they just laughed."

"Who is he?"

"I dunno, but I think Alf can tell us. Anyway, he's near seventeen, he maintains that he can cook, and he says he has first aid training."

There was a silence while the officer contemplated the issue.

"He could be useful, then. It means we have to share the provisions six ways instead of five. It does mean too that we do have an extra hand for watch keeping."

Ben nodded but did not comment further. A few seconds later, the officer said, "What's his name? I need to put it in the logbook."

"Pearson, he calls himself, ain't heard no other name."

He looked at his watch and then said, "Ten past eight. Forty-five minutes to sunset."

"The rain's stopped anyway, that'll improve visibility."

This comment was only acknowledged by an "um" sound.

Had the wind not been blowing from behind them, the two men in the wheelhouse might have smelled the onions being fried in the forecastle, but the forecast breeze was carrying away over the bow the smoke from the stove and the cooking odours. It was first when they saw a figure emerging from the hatch with a plate in his hand that they were reminded of the promised meal. Bert bent down and took a second plate from a hand that reached it up to him. He was used to the ship's movements and made his way on the swaying deck, towards the wheelhouse, with confidence. The same could not be said of the figure following him. Pearson bent low to occasionally grab the low gunnel of the ship as he walked behind Bert, carrying a third plate.

The door of the wheelhouse swung open as Bert approached it.

"Just the job, Bert. Here, Lieutenant, take a plate."

The officer reached over and grabbed his supper. Bert dug his hand into his pocket and took out the cutlery for them. He then turned and took the third plate.

"This one's for Ted. I'll take it down to him."

"So, you're Pearson," said the officer.

The youth looked at the imposing figure in uniform and answered with untypical trepidation, "Yes, sir."

"I want you two to report to the wheelhouse when you have finished your supper, in not more than twenty minutes. Understood?"

"Aye, sir," answered Bert.

Pearson mumbled the same answer and then turned to make his unsteady way back to the forecastle.

As requested, a while later, the hatch door opened and the two of them made their way back to the wheelhouse. Ben let them in. The scene in front of them was a cramped space with some unopened boxes furthest in, the lieutenant's duffel bag propped against them and raincoats hanging on the wall. On the window ledge was a folded sea chart, some navigation instruments, two empty plates, and a pair of binoculars. Ben was at the helm and the officer was standing beside him, no longer wearing his jacket but now a blue jumper with the gold flash emblem of his rank embroidered on.

"Who cooked the supper?" asked the senior man.

Hesitatingly, Pearson said, "Well, I did, sir."

"Well, you can stow away on my ship anytime you want."

There was a pause while the boy tried to understand if this was a criticism or praise.

"Err, thank you, sir."

"How did you make the potato cakes?"

"I made a mash with the dehydrated spud they put on board and mixed in chopped onion that I'd fried."

"Good show. Now, you two have the youngest eyes on the ship and I want some keen observers to do an important job this evening."

Ben was listening intently, but with the instinct of a seasoned sailor, something made him feel uneasy. It was a skipper's sixth sense. He glanced round and, through the single window behind him, he saw the large grey shape of a destroyer. The quantity of white foam flying up from the bow betrayed the fact that the ship was in a hurry.

He interrupted the officer.

"A ship astern, on port side, Lieutenant."

He put on his cap, which had been hanging on top of his raincoat, and stepped out of the open door.

"Hold your course, Captain. It's HMS *Shikari*, an S class destroyer. I don't doubt that they are going to the same place that we are, but at thirty-two knots! Hold your course, Captain."

"Aye, aye, Lieutenant," answered Ben.

THE MISSION OF A "LITTLE SHIP"

"Don't follow them, though, they won't be going through the Looe Channel, with their draft they will be going the long way round."

Ben did not answer, feeling a little irritated that the lieutenant needed to tell him what was obvious.

The officer stood to attention and saluted as the warship drew level. There was a wave from the bridge and a loud toot as the ship responded to the salute.

He came back inside and shut the door.

They all watched the wash from the stern of the ship wallowing its way towards them.

"Hold tight, everyone."

The officer held on to the door handle. Ben was already standing with both hands on the wheel. Bert, also realising what was coming, grabbed the top of the binnacle with one hand and then seized hold of a bewildered Pearson with the other.

The *Bee*, with no ballast in the hold to stabilise her, swayed and heaved violently as the wake of the big ship hit them.

"I get your point about her being a bit tender when unloaded, Captain," said the officer when the ship's motion had settled back to normal. "Right, men, back to what I was saying. Come over here."

They did as they were told, and one stood each side of him as he directed their attention to the folded chart.

"This is where we started from and this is where we are at the moment," he said as he moved his pencil point to a place on the chart. "We are in what is called the Nab Channel."

The two men peered closely at the location indicated.

"If you look over there," he said, pointing, "you can see the Nab tower. It's that round stone building with anti-aircraft guns on top. Usually, it is manned by three lighthouse keepers, but now the navy has men there."

"Why is it there?" ventured Pearson.

"To guide ships into Portsmouth. There is a foghorn and a light, but the light is not allowed to be on in wartime. Captain, can you steer a little closer, please."

They all gazed at the grey, foreboding building.

"Now, looking at the chart, this is where we are heading, the Looe Channel."

He pointed out the position.

"Fine, that's near enough to the tower, Captain. Now steer a course of 100 degrees. Just a little south of east. Full speed please."

"Aye, Lieutenant."

"The channel is marked by two buoys: one red, one green. We have to go between them. Sunset is in ten minutes, and it will take us just under an hour to get to the channel."

"How are we going to find the posts in the dark?" asked Bert.

"That's your job. It won't be completely dark, but if it rains, visibility will be poor."

"So, what do you want us to do then, Lieutenant?"

"In half an hour, I want you, Bert, on deck, together with Pearson. You will take it in turns to climb the ladder tied to the mast and look for the buoys. You can use my binoculars."

"What do we do when we see them?"

"The man on deck hurries back to the wheelhouse to tell us the direction you see them. Do you know your port and starboard yet, Pearson?"

"Err, not yet, sir."

"You have half an hour to learn. Here are my binoculars. Put the strap round your neck. If you drop them overboard, I'll throw you in to find them!"

They both laughed, and then the two youngest crew members made their way back to the forecastle.

The two men were left alone in the wheelhouse. Every so often, the light rain let up and landmarks on the coast became more visible.

"See, Captain, the tower over there, off the port bow? The chart shows it as being to the east of Chichester Harbour. the sun has set at sea level, but just now, between the showers, it is still on that tower."

Ben, who was used to having the wheelhouse to himself and preferred to navigate in silence, just said, "Um" in agreement. Sub-Lieutenant Russell, on the other hand, was not a great lover of silence, and after a while he took the initiative to create some conversation.

"Captain, you mentioned that you once manned a sailing ship. Did you say that it was also called the *Bee*?"

The officer knew full well that this would be a subject that would be irresistible for his companion to hold forth on.

"I did that. I were fourteen when I signed on."

"What kind of ship was it?"

"'Bout the same size as this'n. She were a ketch, that is she had two masts. Built by Hanson's shipyard in Cowes in 1801. She had the record as being the longest serving trading vessel in the British Isles, 124 years!"

"And she was scrapped in 1927 to be replaced by this one?"

"She were never scrapped, just run ashore in the mud half ways up the Medina and left to rot. They said that she were put there to protect the oyster beds."

"Is she still there?"

"That she is. Tis a crying shame, for her timbers are all oak, and they don't rot quick. In her early years she worked for the navy as a supply ship. So, she were around before Trafalgar! Nelson himself might well have known her and even have used her as a ferry."

"That is a real claim to fame. See, there are the lookouts coming out of the hatch," the officer interrupted.

"Looks like Alf has lent Pearson his raincoat," said Ben.

"He needs it too, it's come on to rain again."

They both watched as Bert slowly ascended the ladder, rung after rung, until he was holding onto the top rung with one hand. The swaying of the ship at sea level was significantly amplified the higher up the mast he went.

"We got the force four south-westerly wind over ebb tide, that ain't helping none, she's rollin' some."

"I've seen much worse. In my training at Dartmouth Naval College, we sailed on a full-rigger, the HMS *Britannia*. The movement at the top of the main mast sailing down wind was horrendous."

Ben said, "Um" and returned to concentrating on following the course. But the officer had not finished.

"She was originally 120 guns, first rate ship of the line. Launched in 1820, so not quite as old as the first *Bee*."

Both men had now stated their seamanship credentials and there followed a long silence.

As time passed and the light began to fade, Ben had a growing realisation that they might be motoring into a trap. He decided to express his anxiety.

"We should be real close to the buoys by now. If'nt the lads don't see them soon, we will be too close to the shallows on either side to turn the ship 'round safely to find the alternative longer route, 'specially in the dark."

"Hold your course and speed. We must be very near," instructed the officer, in a voice that indicated clearly that his order was not to be disputed.

Ben glanced at the lieutenant; he could not but admire the coolness of the man as he stared relentlessly through the window as potential disaster loomed. As skipper, Ben always had a reserve plan if things went wrong but, increasingly, the alternative route was becoming an impossibility. If they grounded on the shallows at this speed, they would be wrecked. Despite the insistence of the lieutenant's tone, he considered suggesting that they should slow down. They were just too near the shallows. However, he recognised that the slower they motored, the longer it would take and the darker it would get.

Similar thoughts must have occurred to the officer.

"Slow ahead, Captain. Steady as she goes."

Ben pushed the engine telegraph to pass on the request. They strained to see the men at the bow, but now the rain on the windows had made it all but impossible.

The door was wrenched open.

"Sir, sir, Bert seen 'em."

"Where?"

"He said turn immediately to port otherwise we'll pass the marker on the wrong side."

"Continue slow ahead, Captain, twenty degrees to port."

A moment later, there was a dull thud on the starboard side of the hull, followed by the sound of grating as the buoy scraped along the hull. In the dull light, the men in the wheelhouse could see the top of a red marker sliding by. They were just in the channel!

Waiting until the buoy was astern, Ben answered the angry voice emanating from the voice tube to the engine room.

"What the bloody hell is going on, Skipper?!"

"It's all right, Ted, just a navigation matter. All under control," answered Ben.

"Full speed ahead, Captain. Your course is 80 degrees, that is just north of east. Here, use my luminous hand compass."

"Aye, aye," replied Ben as he pushed the lever on the telegraph.

The door was opened, and though he could hardly be seen in the twilight, Bert stood in the opening with Pearson behind him.

"Your binoculars, sir."

"Well done, the two of you. Go and get some sleep for a couple of hours."

"We can't, sir. We're on watch until two in the morning. Alf takes over after that."

"All right, keep your watch in the bow. Let us know immediately if you hear any other vessels. Tell Alf to report to the wheelhouse when he goes on watch."

"Aye, sir."

The door was closed and the two men inside stood in silence, peering through the rain-streaked windows into near utter darkness, each with private thoughts about the way the other handled what both recognised as the great risk they had taken.

The officer broke the silence.

"I'll update you on the course."

There was the sound of rustling as he took a small torch out from his rain-coat pocket. He flicked it on and shone it on to the folded chart.

"Hold the torch, I need to open the chart a bit. Here you see, the channel. We passed through at 21.15. We sail on this course for an hour and that will take us past the East Borough Head buoy. Then at 22.30 we turn due east. We have clear water all the way to Beachy Head."

Ben studied the chart.

"So where will be at first light?"

"Sunrise is at 04.52, so there should be enough light to see the coast about an hour earlier. Give me the ruler, please."

Ben shone the torch on the window ledge and picked up the wooden ruler. He gave it to the officer, who then took some measurements.

"We should be off Newhaven at first light, and we might see Beachy Head by sunrise. Navigation will be easy for a bit after that if we hug the coast. High water is about 06.00."

"Do you mind taking the wheel? I ought to bring Ted up to date on our progress and show him the chart."

"Good idea. After you have talked with him, I suggest that you take Alf's bunk and get a couple of hours' sleep."

Ben gave his customary "Um" sound, the pitch denoting agreement, folded the chart, and took it with him to engine room.

• • • • • • • ● • • • • • • • • •

It was as the sub-lieutenant had predicted. However, as dawn broke, the sun was not visible from the *Bee*. It was obscured by massive white cliffs, at the foot of which was the lighthouse. The tall building was painted with a broad black band around the middle, as was the very top where the light was situated. During the night, Ben had slept in the watch keeper's bunk for two hours and then gave it over to the officer so that he could get some rest. The man who got no sleep that night was Ted. The two 44-horse-power engines needed his constant specialised attention.

As the ship drew level with the lighthouse, the officer climbed out of the hatchway to the crew's quarters and made his way to the wheelhouse.

"Anything to report, Captain?"

"I seen several other boats, big and small, going in the same direction as us, they all seemed to be in hurry.

"Pass me the chart, if you please." The lieutenant spread the chart on the floor and knelt next to it as he drew a pencil line along his ruler.

He looked up and, pointing down at the chart, said, "Captain, you see my line there?"

"Aye."

"That is a course of 70 degrees, about east-north-east. If you follow that then we will clear Dungeness."

"Um."

"You can turn now, we have cleared the point."

"How far is it to Dungeness?"

The officer put his ruler back on to the pencilled line. After a short while he said, "Thirty-two sea miles."

"So, if we keeps up seven knots, then about three and a half hours."

"That's right. Then we change course to pass Dover. All straight forward. It's after Dover that things get difficult."

"The Goodwin Sands?"

"Yes, and we don't want to be there at low tide. You've sailed through them before, haven't you?"

"I have, Lieutenant. They be right tricky, but the channel is well marked. Have you seen 'em?"

"No, it's new to me, the deep draft warships I sail on stay well out to sea, away from the sands. I once heard that there had been over two thousand shipwrecks recorded there."

Ben turned the wheel to follow the new course. Meanwhile, the officer, still on his knees, continued drawing lines and measuring on the chart. At length he stood up.

"Not good news, Captain."

"Um" with a rising tone indicated that Ben was asking for more information.

"At our present speed, we should reach Dover at around twelve. The Goodwins start just past Deal, which we might reach an hour later, about one or so. That is exactly at low tide."

"Um" with a falling tone indicated clearly that Ben recognised the problem.

"Remember too, we got a strong ebb tide against us just now. It's goin' to take longer.

Chapter 9

THURSDAY 30ᵀᴴ MAY, 14.00 HOURS

It was almost two o'clock when the *Bee* passed Deal; now they had to find a safe channel through the treacherous Goodwin Sands.

"Captain, according to the chart, we should look for a south cardinal buoy that marks the entrance to a channel called Gull Stream, which is safe even at low tide."

"Well, there's one!" said Ben, pointing to a buoy on the starboard side.

"That's it. Keep it on the starboard side. Slow ahead! It looks as if the crew have heard of this area's reputation."

The officer pointed to the men standing in the bow, peering anxiously at the nearby islands of sand created at low tide, when no longer covered by the sea. Alf and Bert were seeing this graveyard of hundreds of ships for the first time. Here and there on the sandbanks were the skeletons of doomed vessels. Unseen by those in the wheelhouse, Ted too was looking at the remains of wrecks, and they passed them while he stood on the step down to the engine room.

Ben pulled the telegraph lever and soon after, the pace of the throb of the engines slowed. The ship crept through the marked channel.

Later, as the channel widened, the scene before them became very busy. There were ships of many different kinds assembled in the deep water outside of Ramsgate Harbour. Most were at anchor, some were manoeuvring to turn east, and several of the smaller craft were following the marked channel into the harbour.

As they motored closer to the motley fleet, a great mixture of warships, fishing boats, passenger ferries, and even pleasure craft, they saw that a fast-travelling naval launch was coming towards them.

"Stop engines, it looks as if they are heading to us," instructed the officer.

The lieutenant put on his cap and stepped outside of the wheelhouse as the launch came alongside. He saluted and then took a line a sailor threw to him.

By this time, Bert had made his way astern. He took the line and held it while Alf hurried to grab a stern line as it was thrown aboard.

"What are my orders, Coxswain?"

The sailor steering the launch barked out his message.

"Sir, the skipper of this ship should anchor at the end of the assembly point behind HMS *Havant,* the destroyer over there. You, sir, are to go ashore in this launch to receive orders for this craft."

"One moment."Although Ben could not have failed to overhear the very loud voice of the coxswain, the wheelhouse door being open, the lieutenant dashed inside to repeat the order. He grabbed his briefcase and then hurriedly boarded the launch.

As soon as the smaller craft had departed, Ben took out his pocket watch. It was five o'clock. They had been at sea for just over twenty-one hours. He looked up and saw Alf at the door.

"Alf, you go down and tell Ted what's a goin' on. Tell Bert to take the nipper with him to get the anchor ready for dropping when we gets past the back end of that fine warship."

Little could they have known that within three days, the destroyer would have been lost, along with eight crew and twenty-five soldiers that had been rescued from the beach.

When the anchor was set, the crew had a chance to meet in the forecastle and have a chat about the last hectic twenty-four hours. In the smoky cabin, the atmosphere was a mixture of relief for a safe voyage and trepidation about what the future held for them.

THE MISSION OF A "LITTLE SHIP"

"Well, that voyage was a real turn up for the books. Still, we made good time, looks like we haven't missed whatever is goin' on here. Not that I see much from the engine room."

"You kept them engines going well, Ted. But I fancy they'll be needed again soon," commented Ben.

"Not least to get us home!" quipped Bert.

"Struth, that reminds me, our families ain't got a clue about where we are. They'll be fretting by now, I should think," said Alf.

"Well, you can be sure the navy won't be tellin' them where we've gone."

"That's for sure, Ted. Pearson, how about getting some grub going. We don't know when we'll have a chance to eat again."

"There's some corned beef tins in them navy supplies. I could do sommat with them, Skipper."

"Bring mine to the wheelhouse, I got to write the log."

"And mine to the engine room, I got to do some checks after that long run."

Just under an hour later, the whole crew were sitting on the hold cover watching the many movements of ships, some arriving and others departing, when they saw the motor launch approaching the *Bee*. Alf and Bert took the lines as it came alongside. The lieutenant climbed on board, but the launch did not depart.

"Let's gather at the forecastle," instructed the officer.

When they were assembled, with a solemn voice he said, "Men, the British Expeditionary Force in Europe is being driven into the sea and our job is to lift as many men as possible from the beaches. This is not going to be pleasant, so if you want to change your mind, do so now. The launch will take you ashore. For those who stay, we leave in an hour's time to cross the channel."

Ben looked round at the crew and said, "Who's for stayin' on board?"

With no hesitation, they all raised their hands, including Pearson.

Ted spoke for the crew when he said, "We ain't come this far to go back home by train."

"Good," said the lieutenant, "the navy has given us two possible routes to get to a place called Dunkirk, where the army is gathering to be picked up. I will discuss with the captain which route we shall take."

As he walked round the hold back to the launch to instruct them to leave, there was a buzz of conversation among the crew.

"So that's what it's all about, then," said Ted.

"And that's what that damned great bundle rope we put in the hold is for," added Alf.

"We'd better get it up before we leave. Ted, please start up the derrick motor and, you others, get part of the hold uncovered to lift it out, while I have a chin wag with the lieutenant."

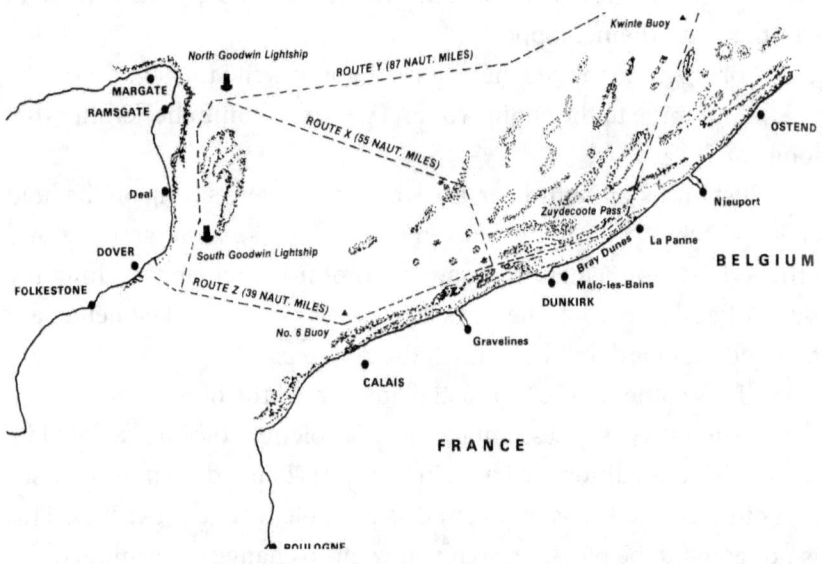

When he got to the wheelhouse, the officer was opening his briefcase. He took out a single sheet of paper; on it was simple black and white chart.

"Captain, in order to avoid congestion and collisions, there are three admiralty approved routes to get to Dunkirk. The shortest, Route X, is reserved for big ships, mainly warships. We can take Y, which is 87 nautical miles, or Route Z. Note by the way, there is a mistake on the chart, the distance is 49 not 39 miles."

"Puttin' aside consideration of distance what's the advantage of one route over the other?"

"The shortest route, Z, takes ships within range of shore gun batteries which, according to intelligence, the Germans have recently taken from the French. Sailing that close to the shore could be risky. We would be within range of the guns."

"And t'other?"

"There are German fast speed E boats ravaging ships on that route. This morning, the destroyer HMS *Wakefield* was torpedoed by one and sank."

"Um."

"You've time to discuss the two options with the crew if you want."

"I'll do that, but I think the shorter option, Z, is best. After all, it will be dark soon after we get to the French coast, so we won't be a sittin' target for long."

"True. Here are some notes I made for you at the briefing I went to this afternoon."

Ben took the piece of paper and looked at it.

"So, tomorrow, high water is at 08.22 and low water at 15.06." He paused and then asked, "What's the tidal range at Dunkirk? The difference in depth between high tide and low tide."

"It's on the notes there somewhere."

The lieutenant looked over Ben's shoulder and then pointed to a scribbled footnote.

"There, we are between neap tide and spring tide, so the range is only about three metres, a fathom and a half."

"Just so I got this right, at high tide, that is at 08.22, we'll have about a fathom and a half of depth, nearly three metres more than at low tide."

"Correct."

"Bearin' in mind that them soldiers will be wading to the ship, at that time we must go really close in shore so they can reach us."

"That is so and the reason why your vessel with a flattish bottom is particularly well suited to this task."

"But once the tide starts to ebb, then we must see to it that we don't get stranded."

"Very true. Remember too that we will be taking on a human cargo, so we must be mindful of their weight affecting how much water the *Bee* needs to stay afloat."

"Um…and how about the weather?"

"Calm conditions overnight and the possibility of enough fog to keep the Luftwaffe away from us until we anchor off the beach. Force 3 north north-west tomorrow, but on the 1st June the wind gets stronger, north-west Force 4."

"Right ho, north, north-west tomorrow will blow us on to the beach, must watch that. I'll talk to the men about the route."

"What are they doing with the crane?"

"Gettin' the scramblin' nets out from the hold, ready for tomorrow."

"Good. How's the new crew member shaping up?"

"Bit rough around the edges, but he might make a sailor eventually."

"Just so you know, should it be mentioned, that a ship from the Isle of Wight, a paddle steamer called *Gracie Fields*, was hit this morning on her second trip ashore to save soldiers."

Ben was shocked; the brutality of war suddenly hit him. He knew the ferry well.

"What happened?"

"I heard about it in the mess hall in Ramsgate. She had 750 soldiers on board and then took a bomb on her engine room, which jammed the rudder and the throttle. She was going round in circles at six knots while the destroyer HMS *Pangbourne* tried to take off her passengers and crew.

"Um." There was a pause. In Ben's mind he saw the colourful paddle steamer and felt sadness that it was damaged. But then he realised his sympathy should be for those 750 soldiers and the crew, stranded on a stricken ship, going round in circles while bombs rained down on the sea.

"Um…so they was all rescued, then. Praise the Lord for that anyway."

"Oh, I almost forgot. I need a 12-volt supply. Can you tell the engineer to come to see me."

"Aye, aye."

Ben returned the notes to the lieutenant and left the wheelhouse to gather the crew. It was a short meeting with no dissenting voices. The route confirmed was Z.

"Ted, can you run a 12-volt supply from the engine room to the wheelhouse? The lieutenant needs it for something."

"You got a supply to the light in there, but maybe he needs more current than that circuit can handle."

While Ted was running a cable from the wheelhouse to the ship's electrical supply, Ben and the officer studied the small map of the routes and related it to the full chart showing more detail of depths and plotted their course.

"We have to turn about and go back through the Gull Stream."

"That's no place to be in the dark, we oughta up anchor as fast as we can," said Ben.

"Agreed. We have just over two hours of daylight left. It is just over ten miles to Dover, so if we leave shortly, we should be there by nine."

"And when we reach Dover, turn east for Calais."

"Another 16 miles, so we could be there well before midnight."

"And how much further up the coast is Dunkirk?" asked Ben.

The officer held his divider up against the folded chart and then said, "About another twenty, we could be there before three in the morning. The sea is quite calm, we must try to get there earlier. My orders state that we should head into the beach at 03.35 at first light."

Ted overheard the conversation and joined in.

"I'd better get them engines goin'. I'll connect this up when we're at sea. Can I ask what you need the electric for?"

"It's for a signal lamp. We must be able to communicate with the coordinating naval ship HMS *Wolfhound* at Dunkirk."

The lieutenant pointed to one on the boxes he had brought on board, which was on the floor in the far corner of the wheelhouse.

"I'll show it to you later."

Ben followed Ted through the wheelhouse door and shouted to Pearson, who was leaning against the mast, watching all the ship activity going on around them.

"Nipper! Kindly ask the others to come on deck for orders."

Pearson was spurred into action and hurried to the crew's quarters. First Bert, and then Alf, quickly appeared in the hatchway and made their way to meet the skipper. Ben briefed the crew about the course plan and told them to be ready to raise the anchor very shortly.

The throb of the powerful engines reverberated through the ship, first a slow "pomp", "pomp" and then it gained in speed as the machinery was wakened from its repose. The wind dispersed a jet of black smoke as the exhaust blasted it out from low down at the stern. After a few seconds the engine rhythm was even, indicating that Ted was ready to set off.

Ben leant out of the wheelhouse and waved to the two men at the bow. He disliked shouting orders, preferring to use hand signals. The men had his attention and saw that his hand lifted from his waist to his shoulder, the signal to raise the anchor. He remained in the doorway watching the bow team's progress. Every now and then he glanced round the area surrounding the ship to ensure that in the busy seaway, there were no ship movements that might present a danger to them or that they might to another.

Alf waived – the sign that the anchor had been broken from the seabed. There was the sound of the chain running through the windlass winch and then a clunk as anchor hit the top of the metal hull and found its way into its resting place. Ben leant into the wheelhouse and pushed the telegraph to "Slow Ahead". He stepped in, grabbed the wheel and turned the ship to port to follow the fairway out of Ramsgate and into the Gull Stream. Several other ships blew salutary toots, God speed blessings, as they recognised all too well where the *Bee* was going. Ben leant out of the still-open door and blew an answering blast on his portable foghorn.

The passage through Gull Stream was uneventful. When they had the white cliffs of Dover in sight, Ben turned the wheel to port – destination: France!"That's it, Captain, we leave the embrace of Mother England behind and venture towards foreign parts and dangers yet unknown."

As the ship swung eastwards, the crew in the forecastle cabin noticed the change of course. One after another the three of them appeared on deck. A glance astern at the massive cliffs showed each of them that the *Bee* was heading for the Continent. They moved amidships and sat on the hold cover, looking at the sea around them and occasionally looking back, perhaps wistfully, though no one would have said so. Indeed, Ben noticed that they were not talking to each other, each keeping their counsel, not speaking of the growing apprehension they were feeling.

As the oldest and more experienced of the three, Alf felt the apprehension most. He had experienced an earlier war and knew of the terrible things that could happen. The cruelty and hate that drove men to wreak unspeakable violence on fellow human beings. It was only a little more than twenty years ago that he was rejoicing coming home safely from the war to end wars, and now it was happening again. Last time was serious enough, but obviously from the little they had been told, this was worse. The British army was in extreme danger of being forced to capitulate. The anger he felt that the enemy he had helped to vanquish was now resurgent gave him the courage he needed to set an example to the two younger crew.

Bert was excited. He could not have imagined, as they motored up the Medina just two days earlier, that the routine voyage would turn into such an adventure. He had never been abroad before and wondered what it would be like. The officer had said that it would be dangerous. But Bert felt sure that the navy wouldn't have sent the *Bee*, an unarmed ship, across the Channel if there was a risk that it might get damaged. The owners, Pickfords, wouldn't have allowed it.

It was too cloudy to see the sunset, but it was obvious that they would soon lose the light. Pearson looked at Bert and caught his eye; they both grinned. They were sharing similar thoughts, but for Pearson this experience was more, much more than an unexpected voyage on an unfamiliar sea. For him it was a completely new and staggering vision of how life could be. After years of a strict routine, up at six thirty, breakfast, sport, classes, housework, supper, bed at nine, day after day after day, thrashings and strict discipline, this new world was full of the unexpected, of excitement and of people who seemed to like him. Though that was perhaps too strong a supposition. His world was one of chipping away at the authority of his teachers, sneering at those fellow pupils who were weaker than him both in body and mind, and occasionally punishing them for it. Always having to watch his back, looking out for those who might threaten him and his money-raising schemes and exploitation of the advantages of dishonesty. This was different.

Alf was like what he imagined a dad would be. The man had listened to his story, a story he had never told anyone since he was in court. Alf didn't wag a finger or threaten. And Bert, well he could have been jealous of having to share space in the crew's quarters, and perhaps he was, but he didn't show it. His friendliness and willingness to help, explain, and literally show Pearson the ropes made him really likeable. He did not seem to resent the new, young crew member. Pearson had nothing to offer him in return for his kindness and the cigarettes he had given him.

And respect! At least Pearson had one skill the other crew already respected him for – he knew how to produce food that was tasty and better than their usual fare. Even the posh officer seemed to enjoy his cooking.

Many new things, but most thrilling of all was the sea! With the memory of his dreadful experience of being wet through and cold while being towed in the open dinghy receding to almost being forgotten, the wide-open space of water around the ship accentuated his feeling of freedom. Alf and Bert had told him of its dangers, but at the moment at least, it made him feel good. And what of this place they were going to? He had seen war films at school; was he really going to have the excitement of seeing the shooting, the bombs, and the killing of the enemy, for real? That was a really exciting prospect.

The only sounds had been the throbbing of the engines as the ship steamed on at full speed and the lapping of the sea as they ploughed through it but, gradually, they all became aware of another sound – the drone of aircraft. Far overhead there were planes heading for England. The dusk signalled the start of the nightly bombing raids.

"Look, look over the stern," said Alf. "The search light crews were waiting for them."

In the dim light, the onlookers were just able to discern the raiders as they crossed the white cliffs that could still be made out in the pale light. Beyond them there were many beams of light appearing, stabbing into the sky with a curious pink colour.

"Christ, there are dozens of planes!" commented Pearson.

"Looks as if they are on course for London."

"I reckon you're right, Alf, it would be due west from here," added Bert.

As they spoke, the booming of anti-aircraft batteries started up and gradually increased in number. The crew sat mesmerised by the distant flashes of the exploding shells, their light intensity increasing as the darkness fell.

"Alf!"

The shout had come from beside the wheelhouse. Alf looked round and saw Ben gesticulating to him to come over.

"Alf, Ted has had no sleep since we left Portsmouth. Go down to see him and offer to keep an eye on the pressure and temperature dials for a couple of hours. We shouldn't be changin' course and speed for a while."

"Aye, aye, Skipper."

"He's a stubborn bloke, you might need to persuade him."

Alf laughed and then walked round to the stern and the entrance to the engine room. The hatch was open, as it often was when the ship was at sea. The air in the busy space got stale quickly and, in any case, smelt strongly of the fuel oil that fed the thirsty Swedish engines.

It was well known on board that Ted considered the engine room to be his domain, and potential visitors had to be invited in.

"Ted, can I come down for a word?"

"Yeah, come on down, Alf. Tell me what you're seeing up there."

Ted climbed down the metal steps. He looked around the engine room and said, "Fair hot down here, Ted, don't it make you sleepy?"

"It do that, but these beauties need constant attention. They keeps me awake all right."

"That's why I come down. Why don't you take forty winks while I take over for a while."

"Ben sent you, didn't he?"

"Well, I can't deny it, but I agree with him. We got no idea when we'll next get a night's sleep."

"Tell you what though, it can get a bit lonely down 'ere, I'd be happy just for a chat with a fellow human being. I talks to these engines and in a sense they answers me, or at least they do through the dials on each one, but tain't quite the same."

"Ben says that we'll keep on this course and speed for a couple of hours, so at least you could have a sit in your cosy corner over there on your blanket, and we can have a chat."

"Let me just make a note in the engine log and then I will."

Alf sat down on the stool that was usually Ted's place, and after a while Ted folded a blanket and sat on the floor, leaning against the only part of the hull not occupied by machinery.

"Well, Alf, what do you reckon of this lot then?"

"Turn up for the books, ain't it?"

"Good to have a chance to do our bit, in my estimation."

"You've already done your bit, though, in France, ain't you?"

"And Turkey before that, like you did. What a shambles that was."

"Yeah, Suvla Bay on Gallipoli, we lost a lot of friends."

"Including Ben's young brother, Harry. He were just seventeen, he lied about his age to get into the army."

"'Course you were a sergeant then.".

"Yeah, Alf, in a machine gun unit and I was transferred to France as such. You went to Palestine though, didn't you?"

"Yeah, we chased the Turks across the Sinai Desert. Mind you, they were good fighters, that's where Ben's sister's husband, Albert, was killed."

"That's right. So now I'm gonna see France again. It was there in the Battle of Arras, in April 1917, that I was promoted to lieutenant."

The conversation continued for a while and then petered out as Ted dozed off. Alf tried to stay awake but also started to rest his eyes. Their peace, if it could be called such with the rumble of the engines, was interrupted by Ben's voice on the speaking tube from the wheelhouse.

"Standby for a change of course."

"Alf was nearest to the tube and responded, "Aye, Skipper." Ted yawned, stretched his arms, and picked himself up from the floor.

"I'd better go up to get orders. See you later."

"Yeah, we will that, Alf. Oh, I forgot to ask, how's the young nipper doin'?"

"He's a bit rough, been a bit of a tough guy I think, but let's give him a chance. He might shape up. I'm a bit concerned for him and Bert too. You and me have seen action before, blood, death, you know what I mean. It's going to be a shock for the youngens."

"Too true, Alf."

Alf made his way to the wheelhouse. Away from the noise of the engine room he immediately became aware of the rumble of big guns, heavy artillery pieces. Opening the wheelhouse door, he said, "Bit of a fight goin' on somewhere, Ben."

"Um…there is that."

Although he could not see the officer in the dark space, Alf was quickly aware of the man's presence when he said, "Seems like an artillery battle between the French and the Germans, or could be the British Expeditionary Force, I suppose."

"Anyway, at least they are not firing at us," said Alf.

"I'm sure the Jerries would if they could see us."

"Alf, we're turning north now, up the French coast to Dunkirk. Should be there before three. As soon as we get there, we'll anchor. Dawn is around half past three."

"All right, Ben, I'll tell the others."

The lieutenant then added, "As soon as we are at anchor, I want the scrambling nets hung over the bows of the ship, so that soldiers can clamber aboard.

"Aye, aye. I'll see to it," answered Alf as he left.

"Captain, my orders are that at dawn we should head into the beach at speed and ground the ship. As I mentioned before, we will be on a rising tide, so the sea should lift us off again in due course."

"Um…understood."

There was silence in the wheelhouse as Ben steered north with the help of the lieutenant's luminous compass. But the help was not really necessary as both men could now see a glow in the sky, the glow of destruction being wrought, to guide them to their destination. In the silence, Ben tried to catch up with his thoughts. Increasingly, they dwelt with consternation about the fact that the families of the crew, including his own, would by this time be extremely worried about where their menfolk were and what had happened to them. Ben knew that their mission was secret and there was no chance that Pickford's would have any information to give the worried wives, mothers, fathers, brothers and sisters at home. But there was another nagging, related issue which worried him. Tomorrow will be Friday, last day of the month. Mae and Amy would have to pay the rent man, the insurance and other things which will be due. They will need money from his pay packet!

After some tortuous thought he realised the solution. Molly was hoping to get married after the summer. She and her fiancé, Ron, had been saving for the wedding. Surely, she would offer to lend the sisters cash from her wedding savings.

He was jerked from his reverie and into reality as a voice beside him said, "Should be there in an hour, Captain. I'll take over for thirty minutes; you get a rest.

Chapter 10

FRIDAY 31ST MAY, 03.00 HOURS

As the *Bee* arrived off Dunkirk, the large fires burning ashore and the first glimmer of light on the eastern horizon revealed dark images of many ships of differing shapes and sizes, all at anchor. Ben chose a space and pushed the telegraph to "Finished with Engines".

As the sea slowed the ship almost to a halt, the wheelhouse door opened and Pearson stood looking in. He had to shout to make himself heard. The rumble of gun fire in the distance and bombs exploding were louder than ever.

"If you please, sir, Mr Alf has asked me to run back and tell him when you want us to drop anchor."

"Good lad, give him my message to do it now."

As soon as Alf was sure that the anchor was holding, the three crew members went to gather up the scrambling nets and to do as the officer had instructed.

"When they have finished with the nets, we need to uncover the hold so that some men from the shore can be put there. How high is the standing room in the hold?"

"Just over five feet, Lieutenant," said Ben.

"It's going to be cramped, too cramped. Men will have to stand in there, if they sit or lay down, they will take too much space."

"Could take the hold cover off altogether, I 'spose. But then all the planks are goin' to take space on deck."

"Right, jettison them and let the tide take them."

"What, chuck 'em over sides?"

"Yes. Please get your men to start as soon as possible so that we are ready to move at dawn."

"I'll gather the crew and tell 'em what the plan is and then get the covers done."

Ben took the lid off the speaking tube and called, "Ted, come forward to the crew's quarters, I've got some things to tell you all."

He left the officer in the wheelhouse and made his way carefully along the deck in the dark. There was a candle burning on the table and the three occupants were sitting around it, smoking.

"Blimey, at last I can have a draw on my pipe. The lieutenant don't appreciate the smell of the smoke," said Ben as he tapped it on the ash tray. "Right, the plan is that at dawn, we weigh anchor and make for the beach at full speed. The lieutenant has orders for us to run the *Bee* into the sand as close to the beach as possible so that the soldiers can reach us. Even so, they're goin' have to wade out."

"Do he know what damage we might do to the hull if we hit an obstruction near the beach at full speed?"

"If he do, he ain't sayin', Ted. It's important that you all grab hold of something solid as we get into the shallows. When we ground with a hell of a jerk, you could be flung into the briney or worse."

"And how do we get the *Bee* off again?" asked Alf.

"We're goin' in on a rising tide, so he reckons that the sea will lift us up enough for us to get out ass afore."

"If we leave goin' astern, you won't see to steer Ben, we'll have to turn quickish so that you gets a view of where were going. There'll be lots of other craft and wreckage I'll be bound."

"Um...happen you're right, Ted. T'other thing he's decided is that we should get rid of the hold cover and ditch the planks overboard. This is to make as much space in the hold as possible. Just keep one plank in case we need a gang plank."

"What, chuck the rest overboard?"

"Aye, Alf. It do make sense, though. Can you supervise Bert and Pearson and set about it now, afore it gets light? Oh and, Ted, when you get to the stern, can you pull the dinghy right up close to the ship so's we don't get it tangled up with other nearby vessels."

"Aye, Skipper."

"I got to get back to the wheelhouse." He hesitated; he knew that words were necessary. "Wishin' you all a successful and safe day and remember: what we're all doin' is a really worthy piece of work." He stopped and then continued, "Didn't get much of a puff on me pipe."

"You should try fags instead, Skipper," joked Bert.

With the anchor set, the incoming tide slowly turned the ship so that it cocked to be parallel with the coast, the port side facing east towards the beach, the direction from where the day was making its debut.

The rising sun began to lift the veil of darkness to reveal the awful detritus of combat. The crew were standing in the bow gawping at the scene confronting them. Alf had his hand on Bert's shoulder. They were stunned as they pointed out to each other the ghastly debris. Everywhere they looked there were signs of death and destruction on a dramatic scale. Bodies, some whole, some mutilated, were floating in pools of blood or oil; the light was not yet strong enough to tell which. Splintered timbers and parts of wrecked vessels bobbed alongside boxes, papers, and unused life jackets. About two hundred feet away from them was the paddle steamer, *Gracie Fields*, very low in the water and showing the damage caused by aerial bombardment the day before.

Ben broke the silence in the wheelhouse.

"I hope we haven't got here too late, Lieutenant."

"Too late for some poor blighters, but not so for those," he replied, handing his binoculars to Ben.

"Glory be, there's hundreds of 'em. A stream of men are coming down through the gap in the sand dunes."

"Look over there, to the right. The docks are on fire; the big oil tanks are burning."

"Um…that must be why we can't go into the harbour to pick men up."

"It appears that one jetty is still being used, there is a British ship lying to there."

Ted appeared in front of the wheelhouse. He looked at the sea for a while. Memories flashed through his mind of the time on Gallipoli when it was his job to crawl out into no-man's land at night to collect name tags of fallen British soldiers. He stepped back and opened the door.

"Lieutenant, we should fish these bodies out and collect their name tags. It's the decent thing to do, so that next of kin can be informed."

The officer replied formally. "Permission denied. Please restart the engines, we have business to do to help the living."

Ben stayed silent. He knew that both men were right, but the lieutenant more so. He stepped out through the door and shouted to the men at the bow.

"You got the scramble nets fixed?"

There was a ragged chorus of, "Aye, Skipper." Ben shouted through the open door, "Ready to go, Lieutenant."

"Thank you, Captain. As soon as the engines are going, give the order to weigh anchor."

Ben climbed back in and waited until the throb of the engines was constant and even. He leant out of the door and gave the signal to Alf for the anchor to be raised, then watched for a while until he saw the hand signal indicating that the anchor was stowed.

"Ready, Lieutenant!"

"To the beach if you please, Captain. Full ahead both."

Ben pushed the lever on the telegraph. As the throbbing increased in volume and tempo, he turned the wheel. The ship joined several others, most smaller than the *Bee*, making for the shallows. Other, larger ships nearby, including the destroyer HMS *Anthony* and the troop ships SS *Normannia* and the SS *Archangel*, were standing by, waiting for soldiers to be brought to them by the fleet now heading for the shore. Out of the corner of his eye, Ben saw a bright flash.

"D'you see that, Lieutenant?"

The officer strained his head to look at where Ben was pointing.

"It's a Very pistol shot from HMS *Anthony*. Like a rocket. A white flare means, 'Danger in a non-emergency situation'. Could be warning us of something."

They had not gone many boat lengths. Alf was crouching down by the anchor windless tidying the lines and the two younger men were standing by the rail, cigarettes in their hands, looking at the jetsam in the sea, when there was a colossal roar overhead from the direction of the stern. The deafening sound of the aircraft at low level was punctuated by a sound that Ted knew all too well – machine gun fire. The men at the bow froze and stood looking at the quickly approaching plane, not knowing which way to go to shelter from the twin engine aircraft as its guns raked the sea parallel to the *Bee*. Remarkably, although the gunner, whom the crew could see, sat in the cockpit beside the pilot with a clear view ahead, his aim was poor and no damage was done. The crew watched as it flew off in a wide circle, fearing that it would return and, next time, release its bombs. Instead, the plane joined others that were overflying the beach and machine gunning the troops there.

The lieutenant was furious. "For God's sakes, Captain, if the crew don't act faster than that and think that they can just stand on the deck having a quiet smoke in the middle of a war zone, they will dead before we get to the shore. They have to be more observant and duck low at the approach of aircraft. That Very flare was clearly warning ships that the incoming aircraft had been spotted."

Ben showed some resentment when he said, "But they weren't to know that, were they?"

"Nevertheless, they need a talking to."

He opened the door and made his way along the deck. Ben soon saw him wagging his finger at the two younger men and, he assumed, telling them in no uncertain language that they couldn't act like spectators if they wanted to survive. The officer left the two crouching with as much cover as the rim of the hold would afford, looking shoreward in readiness for their work to get men aboard. From the wheelhouse Ben could see them pointing out the many grim signs of desperate retreat. Upturned small craft, bodies, whole and dismembered, and personal belongings drifted at the whim of the wind, the waves, and the tide.

Suddenly their attention was directed skywards on the port side of the ship. Ben craned his head to see what they were pointing at. He had hardly time to do so before one of three planes coming towards them, in single file on the port side, released its bomb. The two men in the wheelhouse ducked as it exploded by the side of the destroyer, HMS *Anthony*. The second fell harmlessly into the sea they had just passed.

The third pilot, some way behind the others, clearly had his sights on the *Bee*.

The lieutenant shouted to Ben, "It's a Heinkel 111 bomber like the last one! You can identify them by the transparent dome cockpit at the nose of the plane!" As it dived towards them, the horrified spectators had a view of the German pilot and the gunner intent on their prey. The bulging metal cylinder was released towards the ship. Those on deck threw themselves down as the bomb's trajectory took it over the top of the mast.

It fell no longer than a ship's length from them on the starboard side and exploded as it hit the sea. The shock wave rocked the *Bee* on its beam ends so powerfully that the whole vessel lurched over and scooped up sea water, drenching the three crew members sheltering on the port side. Slowly, to the relief of all on board, the *Bee* righted itself and continued towards the beach.

Another, bigger group of different planes appeared, this time from directly ahead of the *Bee*, but their course was towards the naval warships nearby and their altitude was much higher. The British ships opened fire on the enemy aircraft as they approached. The sound of the guns was overwhelming.

The lieutenant had his binoculars to his eyes as he said to Ben, "That's the destroyers, HMS *Wolfhound*, *Venemous*, and *Anthony* as well as the minesweeper HMS *Hebe*, trying to put them off with everything they've got. They told me in Ramsgate that the *Wolfhound* is the control ship here. It is a heavily armed anti-aircraft destroyer."

THE MISSION OF A "LITTLE SHIP"

"Um, I hope they can knock some of these planes out of the sky," said Ben who was gripping the wheel tighter than usual. He told himself that it was because he anticipated the ship running aground any minute, though in reality, fear played a part in it. As he steered, he kept glancing up at the formation of planes approaching them at great height. The officer was doing likewise.

"I've never seen this before, but I have heard about it. Those are probably Junkers 87, Stuka bombers. See they have a wing shape like a bird. They dive down at great speed on their target, and the steepness of the dive makes them very accurate and difficult for anti-aircraft fire to hit. God help those ships."

"Um, they seem to be sparin' us anyway. God, what's that noise?"

"The Stukas have a siren that makes a high-pitched whine sound as they dive. It's meant to terrify their target."

They both watched and listened helplessly as the attackers descended on the *Anthony*.

As the first bomb struck the destroyer amidships, there was a huge explosion followed by another when a second bomb split the stern open. The bombs from the other planes fell nearby but did no more damage. HMS *Anthony* was left in a dire struggle to stay afloat.

"She's listing badly, can't see her surviving," said the lieutenant.

Ben could not but admire the lieutenant's calmness, and replied, "Happen could have been us."

"Quite, Captain. Hold your course, let's do our job."

But it was not over, another formation of Stukas appeared, and this time their targets were the troop carriers. Of these, it was the SS *Normannia* that received most of their attention. The multiple screaming sounds of the descending Junkers only ceased when their payload had been delivered. Even as those on the *Bee* watched, the old troop ship, which had already survived one world war, received several bombs.

While looking at the ship through his binoculars, the officer said grimly, "There's nothing we can do, Captain, we are too far away, and we have orders to beach this ship. Poor devils, the soldiers on board are jumping into the sea. Some might manage to swim to the shore or get picked up by other boats in the area."

No more was said between the men and they watched the steam and smoke as the *Normannia* rolled over and quickly sank. All that was left in a great pool of black oil was a raft of wreckage and struggling men, those not killed in the carnage when the bombs exploded as they sought something floating to hold on to until they were rescued.

The Stukas regrouped and started to ascend for a second attack. Concentrating on the water beyond the bow of the ship, Ben was distracted by Alf pointing at the sky to the west, shouting, but with all the din around the ship his words went unheard. Ben steered on relentlessly towards the ever closer beach as his companion looked through his binoculars in the direction Alf was pointing.

"Christ! What a welcome sight. Six, seven, eight, nine of them! Hawker Hurricanes, the RAF is here!"

Ben did not need to look; the swarm of British aircraft flew over the *Bee* in front of him and made directly for the group of Stukas as they tried to gain height for another bombing attack. The rattle of machine gun fire could be heard from the sky, above the rumble of artillery and the *Bee*'s engines as they strained at maximum speed.

Within seconds, two of the vulnerable Stukas lost height and began to spin down to the land beyond the beach, a trail of smoke behind them. The Hurricanes flew around seeking other prey and preventing further aerial attacks on the beach for several precious minutes.

The men in the wheelhouse watched the scene in front of them. There were large groups of men over most of the long beach and the sand dunes behind it, generally in good order, all waiting for their chance to be allocated a vessel to board. There were also many vehicles. Dozens of lorries, cars, and motorcycles were being driven into the sea to prevent them being used by the Germans. A brown horse was running up and down the beach, seized with panic in the chaotic situation.

There was a fearsome jerk which, though all on board had been expecting it, caused Ben to be thrown towards the wheel, the officer to crash into the woodwork below the window, and the men on deck to be shunted hard against the metal work.

Ben grabbed the telegraph and swung the lever to "Stop", hoping that Ted had not been injured in the abrupt halt and could respond to the instruction.

The throb of the engines decreased in tempo.

"You alright, Lieutenant?"

"Fine, should have been more attentive, I was watching the planes. How are the men?"

"Well, Ted must be alive, 'cause the engines have been stopped. Look, see, the other crew are all at the bow looking at the soldiers."

"Dear God, what a crowd. See, they are starting to wade towards us. Is the ship sitting fast?"

"Wedged like nail in a plank. We ain't goin' anywhere."

"Unlike the RAF planes, they have turned and are heading back to England."

He pointed at the group of Hurricanes turning west in the distance.

"Why? Just when we needs 'em."

"They are operating at their extreme range here, probably low on fuel by now. Let's go to the bow to help."

Ted joined them as they made their way forward. Men from the part of the beach where the *Bee* had run aground were forming a queue. The first of them were beginning to wade forward towards the ship.

"It's not as shallow as I had hoped," commented the lieutenant.

"Couldn't get no nearer than this," answered Ted. "Can't see how those wounded men are goin' to get up the scrambling net."

From the field dressings, it was obvious that many in the queue were wounded. Some so seriously that they had to be assisted by others.

A group of the soldiers, with the sea up to their chests, reached the bow, rifles slung over their shoulders as well as their packs. The first started to climb up the nets. Crew members leant over the rail, trying to grab climbers' hands to help them.

As the crew struggled to get the first man aboard there was the now familiar roar of bombers.

"Them Heinkels are back," shouted Alf, pointing at the sky.

Three of the planes flew along the beach, machine gunning the easy targets.

The crew redoubled their efforts and, with difficulty, got two saturated men over the gunnel. They were exhausted and collapsed onto the deck.

"Bert, Pearson, take these men aft and help them into the hold."

"Aye, Lieutenant," answered Bert.

"Thank God, here are the RAF again," said Ted, pointing skywards.

"Spitfires this time," answered the officer.

The British planes scattered the Heinkels, but not without cost. There was a bright flash, and a pillar of smoke rose when one of the Spitfires crashed at the northern end of the beach.

Meanwhile, the struggle to get men up the nets continued.

Ted beckoned to Ben and the officer and said, "This ain't goin' to work, Lieutenant. It's going to take ages to get these waterlogged soldiers with all their kit up the nets. And it looks as if we will have to leave the badly wounded behind."

"We have to remember too that all the time we are here, the tide is comin' in and the water is getting deeper for them to wade out to us. Unless we are quick to get them on board, they ain't going to be able to reach us," added Ben.

"That's true, Ben, and we don't want to sit here any longer than we have to, just a sittin' target for a Heinkel's bomb!"

"You gotta remember too that high tide is just after nine. We have to leave well before then, when the sea lifts us off the sand. If we miss that and the ebb starts, we could be marooned here for goin' on for twelve hours waiting for the next tide."

It was a long speech from the generally quiet captain, but its effect was total.

"So, what do you suggest, gentlemen?"

Ted pointed at the mast.

"The ladder!"

"How would you use it?"

"We could saw it in half and lash a piece on each side of the ship, amidship where the gunnel is at its lowest. It would be much, much easier for men to climb a sloping' ladder than tryin' to shimmy up a vertical rope."

Ted's ingenuity quickly won favour.

"Do it, Lieutenant, do it straight away!" commanded the officer.

"Bert, Pearson, help Ted get the ladder down. You got a saw in the engine room, Ted?

"No, Ben, not a wood saw, but I got a hacksaw, that will do it."

Fifteen precious minutes later, there was a half ladder installed amidships on both sides of the *Bee*. The soaking men immediately started clambering aboard, a few with ease, but many were barely able to climb and needed help, while others had to be lifted or carried by willing hands. On the starboard side, the two youngest crew members gave assistance where required to get men over the gunnel and onto the deck. On the other side, Alf and Ted did the same thing.

The lieutenant kept count of the number coming on board while Ben directed the soldiers to where they should stand and wait for the ship to leave. All the while, there were the sounds of gun fire and bomb explosions, the Spitfires having departed and the Heinkels back, tormenting those waiting on the beach and the row of small craft trying to save them. Several smaller ships - pleasure craft, fishing boats and whalers further down the beach - bore the brunt of the bombers' attention. Loading on the *Bee* stopped as a stick of bombs sailed overhead and exploded nearby in the already mangled wrecks. Unable to help, the crew briefly watched the awful carnage as men, most of them soldiers, with the dashed belief that they had been saved, scrambled in amongst the splintered wood and floating corpses to find something buoyant to cling on to.

"Hurry, keep them coming!" shouted the officer. "Leave the wounded, especially the bleeding cases, on the deck at the bow so that we can see if their wounds can be better dressed."

Ben pulled his watch out of his waistcoat pocket.

"High water in half hour! Ted, get the engines ready for departure to Ramsgate."

By this time the hold was full of soldiers tightly packed together and every space around the ship was occupied. It took Ted a long while to push his way through the throng to get to the engine room.

At the back of his mind, though it was much preoccupied with the terror around him, Ben was uneasy. He had not noticed the ship moving at all, as it should if it were floating near the full tide.

Sub-Lieutenant Russell also had a nagging worry. The ship was crammed with men in khaki, and to an observant pilot, must be a prime target. He was sure that those rescued military men must also have this realisation. Would discipline on board this vulnerable craft hold as the delay to leave this wretched shore seemed interminable?

Standing at the top of the ladder on the starboard side, the lieutenant looked down at the crowd in the sea below. Waiting expectantly, some of the shorter men now had the sea up to their necks. "Sorry, we can't take any more," the lieutenant called to them. There were some oaths and many pleas as Pearson and Bert tried to pull up the ladder.

"'ere, Admiral, can't you take this one? He's in a bad way," shouted a soldier who together with another were holding aloft a man with his head, even his eyes totally bandaged.

"Last one then! Bert, put the ladder down to let this one on. It would be a death sentence for him to be left here. Take the ladder up straight after."

"Aye, aye, Lieutenant."

The invalid was handed up and lifted over the side to be taken to where the other badly wounded men were lying. The officer pushed his way through the crowd to the ladder on the port side and gave the same order.

"How many, Lieutenant?" asked Ben.

"A hundred and eighty-six on the starboard side. How many on this side, Alf?"

"I makes it a hundred and eighty-nine. Maybe a few more."

Despite the distractions around them, the crew tried to do the addition sum. Alf was quickest.

"That'd be three hundred and eighty-four."

Bert piped up, "You can tell a man who plays darts regularly, they gets sharp at arithmetic!"

There was the first and perhaps only laugh of the day between the crew.

"Pearson, did you tell the truth when you boasted that you had done a first aid course?"

"I did that, sir, no, I didn't mean I boasted, I meant to say I have done a first aid course and passed near top of the class."

"Come to the wheelhouse with me and collect the first aid equipment I brought on board. See what you and Bert together can do to help the wounded. It'll take us at least twelve hours to get to Ramsgate. You might have the honour of saving some more lives."

"Alf and Bert, stow the ladders against the mast, I'm sure some of the soldiers will help you. We're goin' as soon as Ted is ready," said Ben.

He turned and followed the officer and Pearson as they squeezed their way through the crowd to get to the stern. As they approached the wheelhouse they heard the reassuring sound of the throbbing engines. The lieutenant went in first and collected one of the cardboard boxes he had brought on board.

"Here you are, Pearson, it's a bit of a jumble, I did not have time to sort the supplies before we left. But you'll find plenty of bandages and other dressings."

"Thank you, sir," said the young man as he quickly left.

"Right, Captain, let's go and get off this confounded beach before the Hun get us."

"Aye, aye, Lieutenant."

Ben reached over and took the lid off the speaking tube.

"Ted, are you ready?"

"What did he say, Captain?"

"Not really repeatable, Lieutenant, but he meant 'yes.'"

Ben seized the lever on the telegraph and pushed it to "Slow Astern".

They sensed the slight speeding up of the engine, but after a few seconds the officer said impatiently, "We aren't moving."

Ben pushed the lever to "Half Astern".

"What's wrong?" demanded the lieutenant.

"We're stuck."

"Why, it is just about high tide."

"It must be the weight of the men. I'll try full power."

Ben pushed the lever to "Full Astern".

The engine was now very loud as Ted gave full power. "We got too much weight, she won't shift."

"She bloody well has to shift; we can't stay here for the next high tide in twelve hours!"

Ben pulled the lever back to "Stop". The engines were now slowly throbbing, but the gears were disconnected.

The door was wrenched open and Ted stepped inside.

"This is a fine ruddy pickle, the Admiralty didn't think this plan through too well, did they?"

The officer was about to give a brusque reply when he remembered that Ted was of equal rank to him. He paused, then with more moderated language than he had planned to use, said, "They should have given us a quota of the number of soldiers we could pick up without having the ship need more water than the tide could put under us."

"I've looked at the arithmetic. We have three hundred and eighty-four men on board, plus crew. Say an average man weighs twelve stone, that makes a human cargo weight of over thirty tons! Then you've got rifles, haversacks and heavy boots. Of course, the ship would go down in the water, but someone has damned well miscalculated how much!"

The officer was on the backfoot. "Well of course the boat would ride lower in the water, but we never expected such a weight."

Ben interrupted the argument. He raised his hand and said, "We are where we are, and arguing ain't gonna solve the problem. There be three possible solutions. First off, we offload some of the soldiers."

"We can't do that! What do we do, throw them overboard?"

"Hear me out, Ted. Second, we try shuffling the men, the cargo, round a bit. For example, we try to get as many as possible crammed forward to let the stern lift and try again on full power. If that don't work, we try the opposite – transfer as much weight as we can to the stern to lift the bow. Seems to me that it is most likely that the bow is stuck since the water will be shallower there."

"And thirdly?"

"We….." There was the sound of approaching aircraft as a flight of Heinkels raced along at low altitude parallel with the beach. The men standing on the deck, as one, tried to duck, though there was no space to do so, while the bombs rained down in a line on the edge of the sea. The queues of men waiting in the sea for transport disintegrated into panic as they tried to get back on to the land. The explosions shook the ship, but once more the *Bee* was unscathed.

"We are going to have panic on board if we can't at least explain to the soldiers what the problem is. They must have realised by now that something is wrong!" said Ted.

Ben quickly said, "And thirdly, we have to try to get a tow off the sand."

"That's the best solution but how do we do that? Look at these little ships round here, there ain't non powerful enough to pull the *Bee* in calm water let alone when we're aground," came the repost from Ted.

There was a brief silence, and then the lieutenant spoke.

"The engineer lieutenant is right; we must inform the soldiers what is happening. I'll identify the highest-ranking officer and ask him to deal with spreading the information. There was a major who came aboard, I'll find him. Meanwhile, let's try the second suggestion. I'll get him to help make arrangements to try shifting the weight to the stern as much as possible."

Ben's idea regarding shifting the weight was very difficult to organise; as the decks were so very crowded, it was difficult for men to move. After wasting a lot of time trying to arrange it, the idea was disbanded.

Alf joined the lieutenant, Ben, and Ted in the wheelhouse to discuss what the next move was to be.

The officer spoke. "That leaves us with one other option before we have no choice but to ask for some men to leave the ship. They might volunteer; it could be safer ashore than languishing here waiting for the Luftwaffe to improve their aim. Gentlemen we have to signal to a passing vessel of enough size how desperate is our plight."

"How do you propose to do that?" asked Ted.

The lieutenant bent down to pick up one of the boxes he had brought on board in Portsmouth and started to pull out some packing material. They all watched as he uncovered what looked like a large lantern.

"This, men, is a signalling lamp. While it works best in the dark, it can be used in daylight."

"Let's hope it works, we have to move within the hour, the tide will have started to ebb fast by then," stated Ben.

"Well, we can't stay here much longer. A lot of the soldiers are near exhaustion. Some of these blokes have been walking for days, and standing for any length of time will be impossible for many. We got no water left to offer them either," added Alf.

"And what's left of the rations we took on board in Portsmouth won't go far if we are to sit here for twelve hours," the lieutenant pointed out. He continued, "All navy ships have a fixed lamp, but this is a portable one. Therefore, I need those twelve volts you arranged for me, Lieutenant Engineer."

Ted grasped the red and black wires trailing from under the lamp.

"Yes, I can fix this up easily," he said.

"How do you send the messages, then?" asked Ben.

"Morse, Morse code, it was part of my training. The problem is, we have to pray that there is a signaller on one of the navy ships who is looking in our direction."

This last sentence poured cold water on the growing optimism in the wheelhouse.

"I reckon we should do something else as well."

"What do you have in mind, Ben?" asked Alf.

There was the rattle of machine gun fire as three Heinkel planes, one after another from north to south, strafed the water between the Bee and the beach. An area, which, until a short while ago, was full of the queue of men endeavouring to reach the ship.

The men on the crowded deck, to a man, once again ducked as far as they could in the circumstances, as did those in the wheelhouse when the Heinkels roared close overhead. Then, a palpable sigh of relief could be heard when they realised that the planes did not drop bombs. Then, also to a man, they all looked north to see if the three aircraft were followed by others.

"They seem to be alone," commented the officer. "Look, I must find that major to explain why we are not leaving, before panic breaks out, if we get any more attention from those bombers. Captain, you do as you see fit if you have other ideas."

The lieutenant left and started to push his way through the crowd, to a position in front of the wheelhouse, to make an announcement to try to contact the army officer.

Ted stated what they all recognised, "There's lots of ships, big and small, dashin' about past our stern out here. 'Course the ones big enough to tow us ain't goin' to risk comin' in this close for fear of runnin' aground."

"So, the problem is to get the attention of the bigger vessels, albeit that they's further away. We knows that if you hang a union jack flag upside down, it be a message to other ships that you have an emergency and need help."

"Yeah, but we ain't got a union jack on board."

"That's true, Alf. What we do have is a red duster on the stern flagpole."

"You reckon that hangin' it upside down might attract attention?" asked Ted.

"You got a better idea?"

"No, Ben, I ain't, apart from the lieutenant's magic lantern," answered Ted.

"Let's try it, then. All merchant seamen know that the red duster, the red ensign, has a small union jack in the top left corner of the red flag. If we hang it upside down, the jack would be bottom left corner," said Alf.

"Alf, get the two lads 'ere. Tie the flag on one of the dinghy's oars. They can take turns standin' in the stern, by the flagpole, waving the upside-down ensign at every vessel they sees."

While the lieutenant was doing his job of informing the increasingly anxious soldiers of the *Bee*'s situation, the two younger members of the crew set about doing as Ben had ordered. When the officer returned to the wheelhouse, Ted helped him to set up the signal lamp.

"Now we have to hope that the naval signalmen on the *Wolfhound* and the *Hebe* are looking towards the shore."

Ted watched as the officer, with the door open, standing on the step to the wheelhouse, held the lamp up at shoulder height with both hands and then started clicking the shutter in the front of the bulb to send a morse code plea for help.

While the officer persevered with the signal lamp, there were many willing hands to help with waving the flag. Each time a ship of any size came near the flag was raised and men around it, in full voice, shouted, "Help!" But their shouts, the display of the flag, and the clicking of the signal lamp shutter went unheeded. It was now possible to see flotsam and jetsam around the *Bee* being carried southwards by the increasing current of the ebbing tide. As the minutes ticked away, the anxiety of those on board increased. It had almost reached a point where some on board really were reasoning that they would be safer on land than on a stranded ship. Murmurings reflecting this began to circulate, though they were quickly halted by the horrific noise when a flight of Stukas attacked some British tanks that had recently appeared over the sand dunes.

Suddenly, Bert's face appeared at the wheelhouse door.

"Skipper, there's a tug that has stopped astern of us, about four boat lengths. It's foreign, I think."

Ben forced his way to the stern, together with the lieutenant. Sure enough, a tug flying the French flag had noticed the *Bee*'s plight.

"Skipper, can you give us a tow!" shouted Ben with the loudest voice he could muster.

The lieutenant improved on the volume as he repeated several times, "Pouvez-vous nous dépanner?"

One of the crew of the French ship had a megaphone. He shouted, "pas assez profond!" and then repeated the phrase several times.

"What's he saying?" asked Ben desperately.

"He says, it's too shallow for him to come near us."

"What's he doing now?"

Several of the French crew pointed to the *Bee*'s tender and then mimed rowing.

Ted was now behind the two of them. He said loudly, to make himself heard over the excited babble of soldier's voices, "They want us to row to them and pick up a light line."

"Get Bert and Pearson. They're agile enough to get over the stern and into the dinghy."

Very quickly, Ted returned with the two crew.

"Right, lads. I wants you to row like the devil's behind you over to the French tug and pick up a light line. Bring the end of it back to us, and for God's sake don't drop it."

"But, Skipper, I ain't never rowed a boat," whimpered Pearson.

"Bert will row, you hold on to that rope like your life depends on it."

"'Cause it does," quipped one of the soldiers nearby.

The two of them clambered over the stern, and when Ted had pulled the dinghy close enough, one after another jumped in.

"Get that flag off and pass the oar to Bert," ordered Ben.

As Bert rowed across the short distance to the tug, the Stukas returned. Fortunately, their attention was on the vehicles on the beach and those sheltering behind them.

"Dépêche-toi! Dépêche-toi! Pas assez profond! Little water, little water!" shouted one of the tugboat crew as the rowing boat approached.

Pearson was in the bow of the dinghy. As they came up to the side of the tug, a crew member passed a coil of rope to him. Although the rope looked quite thin, the coil was heavy, and he had difficulty balancing as he turned and placed it on the floor.

"Right, mate, I've got it. Turn round and head back," he said to Bert as he had his back to the tug.

"You sure they've made the other end fast to the tug?"

It was obvious to Pearson that there was a loop round a giant steel cleat on the tugs deck.

"Yeah. Quick, let's get back!"

As Bert rowed, Pearson paid out the rope over the stern. With the weight of the rope dragging behind them, the dinghy was much heavier and progress slower. When they reached the *Bee*, Alf was hanging over the stern to take what was left of the coil from Pearson.

"Put a loop on the end and make fast to the cleat on the stern, Alf, so's we don't lose it."

"All done, Ben. You can tell them, Lieutenant."

He shouted across to the tug, "C'est prêt, monsieur!"

One of the crew on the tug attached the light line to a heavy rope and pushed the end of it into sea.

"All right, pull her in quick as you can."

Several soldiers heard Ben's order and grabbed the light rope.

A few minutes later, the tow line was attached to the *Bee*. Ben waved and stuck up his thumb. The crew members on the tug responded likewise.

"You reckon they will be able to pull us off with the tide this low, Captain?" asked a nearby soldier.

"I've no doubt. These tugs are used to pulling ships many times our weight."

THE MISSION OF A "LITTLE SHIP"

There was a toot from the tug and the smoke from its funnel increased and turned to a darker shade. The French ship manoeuvred so that its position would allow it to drag the *Bee* directly backwards and not sideways. Then it slowly moved forward. The tow line began to lift out of the sea and straighten up.

"Ted, you got the engines ready to take over when he casts us off?"

"All ready, Skipper."

The line between the ships was now almost horizontal.

"She's shifting!" said Alf. The soldiers had noticed it too and there was a mighty cheer and the sound of clapping.

Ben said nothing. He had not voiced his concern that the tow line might break under the huge strain.

Then, there was no doubt. The ship was gently lifting in the swell. The engine sound from the tug increased as the *Bee* was pulled out into what would have been open water had it not been swamped with floating debris.

After a few minutes, the tug stopped.

"Cast off the tow rope, keep the light line attached to it so they can recover it all," ordered Ben.

A large windless in the stern of the tug pulled in the lines. The ship then turned and came alongside the *Bee*, just a ship's length away. Those on the *Bee*'s starboard side could see the name of the tug, *Abeille 26*. There were some cheers and laughter from the soldiers watching.

The lieutenant shouted across to the tug. "Merci beaucoup monsieur. Nous avons le même nom!"

"Oui, Skipper. Il y a quatre remorqueuses ici. *Abielle 26, 27, 28, et 29*. Bon voyage!"

"What did he say then?" asked Ben.

"Captain, it is an amazing stroke of coincidence that the ship which brought us salvation is called *Abielle*. And abielle means bee!"

There were expressions of surprise and some laughter from those within hearing distance.

"In fact, he told me that this *Bee* is one of four French tugs working here, all called the *Bee*, but with different numbers."

"Well blow me down. That's somethin' special to remember and tell the folks when we get home."

"Which could be tomorrow, once we have dropped these soldiers off in Ramsgate," said Alf.

"First we must report to HMS *Wolfhound*, the control ship, to report how many troops we have on board."

"Fine, which one is she?"

"Over there, Captain," said the officer.

Ben turned the *Bee* to the direction he was pointing. As they made their way to the *Wolfhound*, the lieutenant was signalling to the ship.

"Got them. There's an acknowledgement signal," he stated with some jubilation to anyone within earshot.

A few minutes later, he exclaimed, "Captain, they want us to heave to near to the ship and await orders! I have told them how many soldiers we have on board."

Ben telegraphed "Slow" to the engine room and crept forward towards the warship. After a few minutes, but what seemed an eternity to those on board the *Bee*, all anxious to head for Ramsgate, a navy launch which had been moored to the *Wolfhound* sped towards them.

The launch came alongside, and the lieutenant found his way through the *Bee*'s crowded deck to find out what information the launch carried.

An officer on the small boat stood up and leaned towards the lieutenant. He shouted, "Lieutenant, you are to proceed to the French sloop, *Arras*, and discharge your soldiers on to that ship. Then return to the beach to pick up more. Understood?"

"Aye, aye, sir."

"When you go back the beach, don't run aground this time. There are so many pits on the water's edge, caused by bombing, that your ship could break its back if left aground by the tide."

"Understood. Where is the *Arras*?"

"A quarter of a mile to the west. They are expecting you. Good luck!"

The officers saluted and then the lieutenant made his way back to the wheelhouse.

"Captain, not entirely good news for you. No Ramsgate for us I am afraid. We are to take the soldiers to a French warship just west of here, unload, and then return to the beach."

"Um...um..." with a rising tone indicated the captain's resignation to the order.

"Phew, that's a bit of a shock. Not getting home tomorrow then. Best I go and tell the lads," said Alf.

"Tell Ted the bad news first and then get the lads to put out fenders on the port side so that we can go alongside the *Arras*. I'm plannin' to put us on the leeward side of the ship so that we get some protection from the wind and swell coming from north-west. You prepare the stern line and get the lads to do the same at the bow, though I think it likely they will throw us lines 'cause their deck will be higher than ours."

Chapter 11

FRIDAY 31ST MAY, 13.00 HOURS

It took a while to find the *Arras*. The officer spotted her first, using his binoculars. Although she was a French naval ship, her design was reminiscent of a merchant vessel with a high prow and stern and funnel amidships.

"That's the *Arras*, Captain," he said, pointing.

"She don't look like naval vessel, more like a merchant man. Pretty old too, I'd say."

"I remember from our college studies of foreign navies that there was a fleet of French ships built during the Great War, modelled on the British Q Ships. She must be one of them."

"What's the Q ships then?"

"They were heavily armed naval vessels built to look like merchant ships. Their job was to lure U-boats to the surface to attack them."

"There is a party of sailors along the rail between the funnel and the stern. They must be waiting for us," said the officer as he looked through his binoculars at the French ship.

"I gather that neither they nor we want to be standin' still out here longer than we have to. We'd make a good target for the Jerries."

Pearson and Bert were ready at the bow to throw a line to the sloop or collect one thrown to them.

"Look at those Froggy sailors, they all got blue and white striped shirts," said Bert as the *Bee* neared the side of the *Arras*.

"And white hats. They got red pompoms in the top of 'em," answered Pearson.

The *Arras* had hoved to so that the *Bee* could slowly come alongside. As the ships touched, the anxious soldiers could see the lines being thrown down. No sooner had the lines been secured on the smaller vessel than a number of rope ladders were lowered down to the *Bee*'s deck. Many hands grasped out to grab hold and wait for them to be secured safely. As soon as they were, the soldiers closest started to make their short ascent up to the deck and the hoped for safety of the larger vessel.

Despite many loud calls of "Dépêche-tois!" it was nevertheless a slow business as tired men made the climb, most of them with rifles and packs. As this was happening, many eyes frequently glanced at the sky to see if the pair of ships had been spotted by enemy airmen. Eventually, the *Bee* was empty apart from the wounded men at the bow and some soldiers who had stayed to help carry them. The French were well prepared, and a stretcher was lowered down for them to be lifted up to the *Arras* one by one.

"Cast off!" called Ben to the crew. He went inside and telegraphed, "Slow Ahead", and then shortly after, "Full Ahead". The *Bee* turned for the shore. After they had gone a short distance, they passed a launch packed with soldiers seemingly on its way to the *Arras*.

"Alf, get the lads to tidy the ship up a bit. Chuck any stuff left behind over the side. I see there are some coats and a few jackets. We need to make space for the next lot."

"Aye, aye, Skipper. Look out, heads down, here they come!"

Alf was pointing to a flight of six Heinkels coming in single file from the direction of the beach. As they approached, two planes broke out of the formation and made for the area where the *Bee* was motoring towards the shore. The first plane's bomb fell directly in front of the launch. The explosion sent a shower of splintered timber on to the deck of the *Bee*. Now there remained just a stain of blood in the disturbed sea where the launch had been.

The second plane, some way behind the other, made directly for the *Bee*. Those on deck were aghast to watch the fat cylinder dropping ahead of them as it made its way to the ship. It exploded under the bow and lifted the ship almost out of the water, giving the crew the sensation of ascending in a lift. The vessel then crashed back down on to the sea and partly buried itself in it, a green wall of water on both sides, before rising up again to sit squarely in the turbulence and wreckage around it.

There was a silence in the wheelhouse, each man intensely surprised to be uninjured and just as intensively grateful for the little ship surviving such an impact.

"Bugger me! That was the closest we've been to kicking the bucket, Ben. My God, what a bloody awful sensation. I damned well thought she was going down," gasped Alf.

"Looks as if the sea has cleared up the decks for us, Alf. No sign of any stuff left there now."

"She looks to be undamaged," commented the officer.

"Alf, there's goin' be a lot of water in the hold, we took on a lot of sea. Get one of the lads on the bilge pump to drain it out."

"Aye, Skipper."

Ted appeared in the doorway.

"Someone seems to be looking after us Ben, that really was a nasty one."

"'T'was that, Ted, but may not be the last."

"Damned fortunate that we were in deep water, the sea took much of the shock of the explosion. Had we been further in, in shallower water, we'd have been split wide open."

There was a long pause while they contemplated their good luck and wondered how long it could last.

"How are you two thinking we should pick up the troops now that we can't run onto the shore?" asked Ted.

"What do you think, Lieutenant?"

"I think we will have to use the tender and row round picking them up."

"Um…goin' to take a long while that way, but I can't see how else."

The *Bee* continued towards the turmoil on the beach and then dropped anchor as close in as the captain dared without the risk of grounding.

"Low tide is at four thirty, but there should be no risk of us touching the bottom this far out. The problem is that it is a long distance for us to row in and out collecting soldiers."

The officer was stating the obvious, but as there was no alternative, the crew took it in turns, two at a time to take the dinghy to the shore with all the risks that involved, and bring soldiers back, four at a time. The work was laborious for the rowers and all those on the *Bee*, including the officer who took turns to do the rowing.

As the tender neared the ship, Ben, in the wheelhouse stated, "That's sixteen so far."

"In two hours! Sitting here, sooner or later one of the planes is going to get us," commented the officer.

While the ship was not anchored, it kept as far as possible in the same position so that the men rowing the tender could find it among all the other craft, large and small swarming around in their quest to pick up soldiers.

Suddenly, there was an explosion nearby that narrowly missed a French fishing boat.

"Where the hell did that come from?" commented Alf. "There weren't no planes above just now."

There was a second explosion, causing a column of water to rise up between the *Bee* and a naval launch.

"It's artillery! We are being shot at from the shore!" said the lieutenant loudly.

There was a silence as they contemplated this new danger, then the door opened and Ted appeared.

"That's field artillery, the explosions sound like 105mm howitzers. That's what the buggers used to bombard us with in the trenches," called Ted through the doorway.

"That must mean that the Germans are so hot on the heels of the troops on the beach that they can reach them and us with shells!" commented the officer.

"Must be random firing, we're not in their sights until they get near the beach. Them howitzers has a range of nearly six miles, so they can be some way off yet," added Ted.

"Let's hope so, but it's another nuisance," understated Ben.

"Mind you, knowin' the Germans, they probably will have recognisance information from them Henkels about which way to aim for most result."

"Um…that so, Ted?"

"Look to it, there's a naval launch comin' alongside," said Alf as he hurried through the doorway, quickly followed by the officer, hastily putting his cap on.

As the engine was cut to stay in position level with the *Bee*, one of the three men on board stood up. The coxswain saluted and shouted, "Sir, we seen your tender runnin' a taxi service from the beach and we've come to offer our help to speed things up a bit for you!"

"Excellent, Midshipman. That would be a great help."

"If you hold your position here, sir, when we come back, we'll throw our lines to you and unload on your port side."

"Understood, we will stand by for you."

The launch left and headed for the shore.

Not long after, there was another distraction for those on board the *Bee*. Five Spitfires appeared from the west and immediately flew into a flight of Henkels making their way out from the shore. All the crew on the *Bee* watched the ensuing dogfight and cheered as first one, and then a second enemy plane lost altitude with a trail of flames and crashed into the sea. The remainder of the Henkels turned and made for the land beyond the shore, safe in the knowledge that the Spitfires limited range would prevent them from being chased further.

"Here they come. Standby to take their lines," the lieutenant shouted to Bert and Pearson.

The launch came alongside, and after a while seventeen soaked and weary soldiers joined those already collected by the tender.

THE MISSION OF A "LITTLE SHIP"

The launch cast off and headed back to the shore. As the launch made its way through the increasing number of small boats and the navigational dangers presented by both the floating wreckage and the sunken vessels, the warplanes appeared again from the east. This time they concentrated on the beaches and flew low, machine gunning the teeming crowd of unprotected soldiers.

Twice more the launch delivered full loads of soldiers to the *Bee*, but as they left for the shore for a fourth run, a bomb exploded in the sea by the side of the boat and it capsized, throwing the crew into the sea.

The crew watching from the *Bee* were relieved to see that the men in the water were all alive and seemed to be able to swim.

"Shall we get the tender to them?" asked Alf.

"No need, there's a French motorboat on its way," said the lieutenant. After a few minutes the four naval ratings were safely on board the French vessel.

"There goes our taxi service," commented Ben.

"Yes, we'll have to go back to using the tender," answered the officer as he abandoned his cap and hung it up. "Too hot for that today. The sun is really making it uncomfortable for the men out there on deck."

"Yeah, them uniforms weren't designed for this weather," answered Alf. "I'll get Bert and Pearson into the tender to get another load."

"No, I think it best we get these men offloaded; we have at least two hundred, and some have been on board for over two hours and we have no water to offer them."

"Where do you want them taken?" asked Ben.

"Make for HMS *Wolfhound* and I will use the lamp to ask."

An hour later, the *Bee* was back in position near to the shore, having offloaded the soldiers onto a small coastal freighter which, then being full, set course for Ramsgate. While they were waiting for the tender to return, more and more Belgian and French fishing boats began appearing. Some started to pick up troops near the beach and bring them to the *Bee*.

As they waited for the return of Bert and Pearson in the tender, the lieutenant was using his binoculars to survey the action in the harbour, where one berth was undamaged and was being used to load larger vessels.

"See, the hospital ship *St Julian* has laid to inside the harbour to evacuate the wounded. She's a passenger ship that has been converted," he said as he handed Ben the binoculars.

"There's a shell landed just by her," said Ben, "but it don't appear to have done damage."

"Here comes the tender, tell Alf and Ted to help the soldiers aboard and then take a turn at the oars."

"Aye, aye, Lieutenant."

"Good God, here come the bombers again. Get them on board as fast as you can."

As they unloaded the tender, the *St Julian* swept past them, heading for Ramsgate. Another hospital ship was waiting to take its place in the harbour.

The tender set off for the shore once more, and the officer returned to surveying the action on the beach and the harbour. As he watched the tender reach the shore, there was a series of explosions as the bombers attacked the large ship in harbour.

"I saw the name of that ship when she passed us, she's *Lady of Mann*, also a passenger ship. From the Isle of Man I suppose. It looks as if they just got some damage from the bombing. The crew have fire hoses out. Men are boarding anyway, some on stretchers."

By early evening, with another three hundred and ten soldiers on board, the *Bee* was instructed to unload them onto a freighter, which then set sail for England. The frequency of air raids decreased, but the shelling from the shore grew in intensity. Nevertheless, as darkness fell, they unloaded another hundred men onto a larger ship.

But the night gave no solace. Planes flew overhead, dropping flares to aid the bombers to find targets. The process of rescue continued by the same light and in the four and a half hours before dawn, the *Bee* lifted another hundred and fifty men from smaller craft.

As the time approached when they would have had breakfast, the captain was alone in the wheelhouse with the naval officer.

"Pearson has opened the last can of the bully beef. He is sharing it out between us. No tea I'm afraid, Lieutenant. Alf has two bottles of brown ale, and he's offered to share them, but we got no water."

"Next time we get near to *Wolfhound*, I'll ask if they can lower a jerrycan of water to us. That ship now coming out of the harbour is the SS *Scotia*, yet another passenger ship and a big one. She passed us yesterday. The other ship, the paddle steamer we saw that too, I didn't see the name."

"She'd be the *Whippingham*, the ferry from Ryde to Portsmouth."

"And well overloaded, see how low she is in the water."

The sun was now quite high in the eastern sky, another hot day in prospect. The men in the wheelhouse were each immersed in their own thoughts about what the first day of the new month would bring when a shadow fell over the deck. They both noticed it and looked out the window.

"Blimey!"

"Hell's Bells, Captain. Just when we thought it couldn't get worse!"

They both tried to count the swarm of aircraft between the ship and the sun.

"Must be at least fifty Junkers. God help us all!"

The guns on the destroyers opened up as the ships suddenly accelerated and started twisting and turning in the sea to avoid presenting an easy target to the oncoming hoard.

The planes in the front row of the formation began their dive towards their prey, the horrifying screams of their siren devices getting louder and louder as they plunged downwards.

To the west of the *Bee*, a destroyer was the first to be hit.

"What time is it, Captain?"

Ben took out his pocket watch.

"Eight ten."

The officer scribbled in his notebook and then picked up his binoculars and continued surveying the scene.

"I see it is HMS *Ivanhoe*, and judging by the smoke, that's surely the end of her. HMS *Havant*, the ship we had anchored behind in Ramsgate, is going to help her."

The lieutenant kept a commentary going about the terrible scene around them.

"Oh my god. The *Scotia* has been hit. And again, and again, and one more. There are two Henkels strafing the survivors who are trying to get off the ship before she goes down. Hell! There she goes, turning on her side. Three other ships are trying to fend off the Henkels with their guns and pick up survivors. God, they are jumping from the side into a huge pool of oil!"

"What's that one over there?" asked Ben.

He turned to look at the ship to which Ben was pointing.

"HMS *Basilsk*! She has stopped, must have been immobilised by bombs."

As he spoke, a tug rushed past them in the direction of yet another stricken destroyer. They saw its name, *St Abbs*, as it chugged at full speed.

"It was full of soldiers, where is it going?" asked Ben.

"Towards that destroyer over there, I can't make out the name, but she has obviously been hit. The tug must be going to try to tow it."

As they watched, the awful scream of a Junkers got louder, and the plane quickly became visible to them as it flashed past the *Bee* in a steep descent. The bomb hit the tug amidships. When the smoke and spume cleared, all that was left was a pool of black oil.

"Poor buggers, not a sign of a survivor."

"And they aren't going to be the last, Ben. See, that minesweeper over there, it's the *Skipjack*. There are several planes attacking it. Oh no! One, two, three, four bombs. It's already settling down into the sea."

"And that French destroyer is takin' a beatin'!"

They watched it turn turtle with men swimming desperately away from the hull before it went down and sucked them with it.

There was a tremendous crash. The *Bee*'s charmed life was over. Machine gun bullets smashed into the uprights on the wheelhouse as the two men dived for the floor. A bomb exploded in the sea on the starboard side, and metal splinters tore through the rescued soldiers who were cowering for shelter at the stern. One man, with his face split open, tumbled into the sea. Another bomb on the port side rocked the ship on its beam ends, crew and rescued soldiers grabbing hold of anything firm they could find to steady themselves from going over the side, as the rush of air from the explosion sucked the breath out of their lungs. As the ship righted itself, they saw the paddle ship, the *Brighton Queen*, steam past to find refuge in the open sea. It was crammed packed with black French troops. A Junkers had also seen it, and the escalating shriek announced that it was diving to make a kill. And a kill it was. The bomb hit the mass of troops amidships and a terrible gore rained down on the soldiers on the *Bee*'s deck as it heaved and tumbled about in the troubled sea.

While all this was happening, there was a continuous roar of gunfire from the warships as they desperately tried to save themselves and others. Nor was it in vain as several Junkers pilots would never fly another sortie. But neither could it stop them, as wave after wave of planes arrive to add to the destruction in the sea. By midday, the men in the wheelhouse had seen the destruction of five destroyers, four British, and one French, as well as a minesweeper and dozens of smaller craft. The *Bee* was surrounded by wreckage: wooden French and Belgian fishing boats that were refusing to give themselves to the sea despite their decks being overwashed by it and small ferries and pleasure boats in flames. Bodies, some whole, many mutilated, floated in the jumbled carnage. The watchers on the *Bee* had become numbed by the scale of loss of life. It was a scene beyond imagination. Yet, it was all around them. The sights as desperate men clung to wreckage in pools of black oil, calling for help, and the sounds through the rumble of gunfire of others screaming with pain from their wounds. Small boats were going round trying to pull men from the water but many, slippery with a coating of oil, slithered back into the sea as rescuers tried to hold them.

"Here come some more, Captain," said the officer, pointing at a formation of bombers flying out from land.

"High up ain't they?"

They both watched as the formation kept their height and flew over them.

"Seems they have business further out at sea, Lieutenant. Shall we get about liftin' out some more soldiers?"

"Yes, indeed. Low water is just after five, a good time for the smaller craft to pick up from the beach. Let's move a little further away from the big wrecks in case the Luftwaffe decide to come to finish them off."

"Aye, aye."

Ben lifted the lid off the voice tube and called down to the engine room, "Ted, we're moving a bit and then we'll start looking for a few more soldiers."

There was a muffled, "Aye, aye, Skipper" and the sound of the engines revving. Ben telegraphed "Slow Ahead". After a few seconds, the hastening of the pomp, pomp sound of the engines began to die down.

"Um…sommuts up."

"What do you mean?"

"I means, that we ain't moving," said Ben tersely.

"But the engines were running."

Ben went back to the voice tube, took off the lid once more, and called, "Everythin' all right, Ted?"

"No, it bloody well aint! The port engine clutch jammed when we moved away."

"'Ang on, I'll come down."

Ben left the wheelhouse and hurriedly pushed away through the crowd of soldiers to the engine room hatch. He opened it and climbed down the steps.

"What's this with the clutch, Ted?"

"I'm havin' doubts myself. I'm now of a mind that it's not the clutch that is is faulty, but summat is stopping the propeller from turning."

"What! You mean we have a prop wrap?"

"Possibly. There's so much junk in the water that we might have got somethin' jammed round the propeller."

"Is the starboard prop all right?"

"Seems to be. We can move on that, but if that picks up the same stuff and jams, we ain't goin' anywheres."

"Can you try to put the port engine into reverse to try to shed the junk?"

"That's an idea. Hang on, I'll try."

Ben watched while Ted stepped over to the port engine, revved the engine slightly, and then put it into gear. There was a loud screeching sound.

"That's no good, then," he said as he lowered the engine speed.

"We need to find out what's causing it."

"Well, we ain't going to get a diver out here, are we?"

"Leave it with me, Ted. I got an idea."

Ben went back on deck and with difficulty made his way through the crowd towards the bow. He found that Alf and Pearson were helping some French sailors aboard from a fishing boat.

"Pearson, you boasted about bein' able to swim, according to Alf."

"Er…yes, Skipper."

"Can you swim underwater?"

"For a short time, yes."

"Come with me. Alf, get Bert to take over for Pearson."

When they got back to wheelhouse Ben said, "Come in, Pearson."

"What's the trouble? What's going on?" demanded the officer.

"Right, Lieutenant, here's the situation. It would appear that we have picked up some junk from the sea. Small wonder the ways things are."

"On both propellers?"

"We don't know, but it seems to be only on the port side. Young Pearson here is goin' over the side to take a look at it."

"Can he swim underwater?"

"He claims to be able to. Right, get undressed, lad, you only need your underwear on. Leave your overalls here. Quick, get a move on."

Ben once more made a passage through the crowd of soldiers, with Pearson behind him. When they got to the engine room hatch, the door was open.

"Ted, give me a coil of that light rope, will you."

Ted came up the steps and handed it to Ben.

"Right nipper, I'm putting a loop of this round your chest, knotted with a bowline to hold you. I'm holding the line in case the current gets you or you need hauling out. We need to know what is round the port propeller."

"Do yer know which is port, lad?" asked Ted.

Pearson hesitated and then pointed to the land.

"That's right, don't forget it. And while you're in the water, check the starboard propeller too," added Ted.

"Move aside, please!" shouted Ben to the soldiers as he pushed Pearson through the throng.

"Can you jump in?

"Yeah. How do I get back in the ship?"

"There's plenty of men here to lift you."

Pearson stood by the stump of the stern flagpole, the remainder of which and the flag were hanging over the stern, relics of the machine gun attack. He took a deep breath and jumped. Ben let out the line, looking over the stern as the lad splashed into the water.

"You all right, Pearson?" he shouted.

"Yeah," he said as he shook his hair, wiped his eyes and looked around. Another deep breath, he put his head down and dived.

Very soon, he reappeared. He shook his head to clear water from his face and then shouted, "It's impossible to see anything, the water is too cloudy.""Try again. Can you try just to feel round the propeller?"

"Aye, aye."

He went down again. This time for a longer period. Many heads were hanging over the stern waiting for him to reappear. When he did, he shouted, "I found the propeller, but didn't have breath enough to feel it. I'll try again."

He took his third dive. Ben was getting anxious and kept looking up at the sky, fearing the attention of the Luftwaffe.

Pearson reappeared. Jubilantly he shouted, "There's some really thick rope with wire round it, wrapped round the propeller."

"Good lad, can you get it off?"

"I'll try."

Down he went again. Next time he appeared, he was less jubilant. "It's impossible. It's too stiff and heavy."

"Have a feel of the starboard propeller and see how that is."

"Aye, aye!"

Pearson was clearly enjoying the challenge, and the attention, as he dived for the fourth time.

There was no disguising from the soldiers nearby that the *Bee* had a problem. Many had heard Pearson's report about the port propeller and the news quickly spread among the men crammed together nearby and then further on. This dive, he spent longer under the water. Even to the extent that Ben began to get anxious that he might be in difficulties.

When his head eventually popped up, he held a hand up with the thumb raised and shouted, "There ain't nothin' on the other propeller." A cheer went up from those who could see and hear him, a cheer that spread around the crowd in the stern and continued along the deck. Relief flooded over Ted and Ben, for they knew that if they lost power altogether, the result would be that they would be completely helpless and totally vulnerable, unless and until they could be towed. He tautened the line in his hand to bring the swimmer round to the middle of the stern and then Pearson grabbed two of the many hands being offered to drag him back on board. As he stepped on the deck, many attempted to slap his back and a few shouted comments: "Well done mate"; "Good work, sailor"; "Good lad" and so on.

"Get your clothes and go to the crew's quarters to get dried. Well done, nipper. Ted, can you come to the wheelhouse? We'd better discuss this with the Lieutenant."

When they reached the wheelhouse, the officer asked brusquely, "Well, what's the damage?"

In measured tones, his mouth dry from lack of water, Ben replied, "It's like this. We have a hawser wrapped round the port propeller. The starboard propeller seems to be clear. So, we can move with one engine."

"Well, not all bad news then."

Ted intervened and said hoarsely, "It might be. We have the hawser end round one propeller. Question is, what's on the other end."

"How do you mean?"

"What I mean is, the other end of the hawser might still be attached to the ship it belongs to, a sunken ship."

"Oh, dear God, it would act as an anchor!"

"Precisely that, Lieutenant."

"The only way to find out is for us to try movin' from here. But awful slowly," said Ben.

"Right, let's do that then."

"'Course you have to have a mind to the fact that even if we are free and the hawser ain't attached to summat, we will be draggin' whatever length there is of it, where so ever we go," added Ben.

"One thing at a time, then. Let's establish whether we are stuck to this spot with a hawser attached to something very heavy, like a sunken ship."

"Aye, aye. All right, Ted, starboard engine, slow ahead, when you're ready."

The engineer left the wheelhouse and made off in the direction of the stern. Soon after, the tick over the sound of one engine got louder. Ben took the wheel and mentally plotted a possible course through the forest of obstacles in the sea.

The sense of urgency amongst those soldiers crammed in the area nearest the stern, a feeling that had been relieved when it was discovered that the starboard propeller was not jammed as well, began to return when it was realised that the ship was still not moving. This sense of anxiety was spreading throughout the ship. The lieutenant recognised this and shut the wheelhouse door so that conversation inside could be kept confidential.

"She's movin'," Ben said softly. "But we might just be takin'n the strain on the hawser."

Shortly after, he quietly announced, "No doubt about it, we're goin' forward."

"Glory be," muttered the Lieutenant.

"Amen to that. But we're carryin' some weight on the port side, she's tryin to take that direction. Part 'cause the starboard engine is drivin' her that way and part 'cause of the weight of the hawser."

"But we can move, anyway!"

"So, let's pack a few more souls on the *Bee*, while we got the chance!"

"Yes, looking at the beach just now I could see that they are getting a real hammering from artillery shells as well as the attention of the Henkels. Let's stop here, so that small craft from the shore can find us."

"And any survivors from the stricken ships," added Ben.

"We are within sight of HMS *Wolfhound*, I'll send a signal about our mechanical problem."

Ben signalled "Standby" to the engine room and then left to tell Alf and the others of the situation and to ready themselves for more soldiers to come aboard. He had not passed midships when he found them helping some sailors out of a rowing boat that had come alongside.

"They're covered in oil, Skipper, and fair exhausted," said Alf.

"They say they're from HMS *Skipjack*."

As they watched, one of the last two slipped and fell through the moving gap between the small craft and the *Bee*. He was out of sight, under the gunnel, but screaming for help.

As Pearson started to undo the buttons on his boiler suit, Ben grabbed his hand.

"No, lad, we needs you here."

One of the newly rescued sailors jumped from the deck into the sea and started swimming towards the gap where his comrade had fallen. Many heads craned over the gunnel to watch the scene.

"He's got him, he's holdin' him up!" shouted Alf. "But that oil ain't makin' it easy."

Bert leant over the side while others held his legs and managed to grab the rescued sailor's wildly waving hand.

"It's too slippery!" he shouted.

The rescuer tried with great effort to lift the man up high enough for Bert to grab the man's shirt. Other hands helped and soon the victim was lying on the deck breathing in as much air as he could.

Ben looked over the side to see the rescuer.

"Where is he? He ain't to be seen."

Others lined the gunnel, looking for a sign of the rescuer. But there was none.

Alf shook his head and said, "He's gone, Ben."

"Tragic, he saved the sailor but got drowned himself."

He exhaled loudly and then said," What's happenen' now then, Ben?"

Ben took the crew aside and in a quiet and, because of the dryness of his throat, raspy voice, explained the situation with the port engine.

"So, let's get about fillin' up the ship, lads. And Pearson, I know it don't feel good, but it weren't up to you to go over the side, one man's lost, but we got a job to do to save many more."

"Aye, Skipper."

Ben made his way back to the wheelhouse. There he found the lieutenant signalling to the *Wolfhound*.

"We have orders to take the men we have on board back to Ramsgate, with as much speed as we can get from one engine."

"But we ain't full yet!"

"I know. Captain, have you ever heard of the Battle of Copenhagen?"

"Can't say as I 'ave. Why?"

"It was in 1801. Vice Admiral Horatio Nelson was signalled by his commander to cease his attack. He put his telescope to his blind eye; said he saw no signal and continued the attack that ultimately led to victory."

"So, I take it that we ignore the order and continue to pick up some more men."

"If you say so, but I will of course blame you for insubordination if I get court marshalled."

"But the Royal navy has no say about what a merchant sailor does."

"Precisely."

Chapter 12

SATURDAY 1ST JUNE, 16.30 HOURS

Both men stood in silence in the wheelhouse, watching the crowd of soldiers on deck below them stoically suffering discomfort in the sun. A French trawler was alongside. Alf and the other two were helping soldiers to climb aboard the *Bee*. Periodically, the officer in the wheelhouse reached for his binoculars and scanned the beach and the harbour.

"There's another hospital ship going alongside the harbour mole, the SS *Paris*. We've seen her before. This must be her second or third crossing."

"A French one?"

"No, in fact she is British. By the way, I had instructions about our passage to Ramsgate."

"What did they say?"

"We are instructed to take Route Y back to Ramsgate, the northerly and by far the longest one, eighty-seven sea miles. The signal from *Wolfhound* also gave me orders to report for duty ashore as soon as we get there."

"Why the long way back?"

"The Germans have laid mines on the other two routes. The *Bee* is not degaussed so it would be very dangerous to take the shorter routes."

"De what?"

"The naval ships have a system that produces a magnetic field to counteract to zero the magnetism produced by the ship. The German mines are set off by magnetism. Thus, the naval ships are protected, but merchant ships are generally not."

"Um...did they give you a weather forecast for the North Sea?"

"Yes, wait, I've written it in my log." The officer took his notebook off the shelf and flicked it open.

"For tonight, nor, nor west, force 4, cloudy, visibility very good, warm. For the tomorrow, 2nd June, west, force 3, visibility good, broken cloud, warm."

"No problem there, then, though the contrary winds may slow us."

All the while they had been talking, the crew were taking more survivors on board. Glancing through the window, Ben saw Alf making his way through the crowd towards the wheelhouse.

"That's it, Skipper. We are well full. Not so many this time but the wounded ones have to lie down, it takes more space."

"Fine, we're goin' to Ramsgate with our passengers."

"Really! I suppose that's good news, but there's still need for us here."

The officer interrupted and said, "Admiralty orders, Alf. I can see the reason. If we're dragging this hawser around, sooner or later it may get tangled on a wrecked craft and then we are done for. However, getting to Ramsgate won't be easy. For the safety of the ship and our passengers, we have to go the long way round, the northern route. Since we can't make more than four knots on the one propeller, the eighty odd mile voyage will probably take at least twenty hours, probably much longer, depending on how we get slowed down by what we are towing."

"I'll go down to tell Ted. We'll sail south past the harbour and circle round all the wrecks to find clear water, before we turn north," added Ben.

"The young lads are about all in, but they will take some persuadin' that we can't help more."

"You'll have to explain to them, Alf. You can spread the word among the soldiers that we are shortly heading for Ramsgate, but that it will be a long, slow voyage, partly through the night," added the officer. "Um, one more thing, I have heard a rumour that you are hoarding two bottles of brown ale. Can you smuggle one of them through the crowd for the crew in the stern to get a taste?"

Alf laughed and said, "Share and share a like, sir. Shall be done."

Soon after, Ben signalled on the telegraph, "Slow". He turned the wheel to head south, but as he did so he saw a ship's lifeboat ahead of them. There was one sailor sitting on a thwart. Though his white hat was missing, his shirt showed that he was French. He was waving frantically at the *Bee*.

"We can't leave him. Standby, I'll try to drift up to him," said Ben after sending the message "Stop" to Ted.

Ben used the momentum of the vessel to slowly approach the lifeboat. The Frenchman was still gesticulating and shouting towards the *Bee*.

"I'll go and see if they need an interpreter," said the lieutenant.

Ben watched as the stranded sailor held out an oar for one of the soldiers to catch hold of to pull the boat towards the *Bee*. When it was alongside it was made fast. The sailor was pointing at the floor of the boat and as he did so, unseen by Ben because of the crowd, another crept out from under a thwart, then another until there were five of them imploring to be taken aboard the *Bee*. They climbed over the gunnel, and the lifeboat was cast adrift.

"Who are they?" asked Ben when the officer returned.

"All of five of them were part of the crew of the *Foudrayant*, the French destroyer that was sunk earlier. They had been hiding under the thwarts to try to avoid being seen by aircraft."

Ben turned and pushed the telegraph once more to "Slow".

"I'll speed up when we are clear of the danger from floating debris," he said.

But they were not to be left in peace. As they passed the harbour, directly ahead of them was a flight of Junkers, obviously on their way to attack the harbour.

"Must be about twenty of them, Ben. Look! One has peeled away from the others and has caught sight of us!"

"Um…" he murmured as he reached for the telegraph and pushed the lever to "Full". "Our only chance is to swerve to starboard and hope that the bomber can't turn towards us once he's started his dive. But we got precious little speed with one engine."

The dive bomber's screaming sound was unnerving many of the troops on board, but there was no cover for them. Fixated, most just watched as the plane levelled its dive and released four bombs. All on board could see the egg-shaped containers sailing through the air. And then a tremendous crash as they hit the sea, the nearest about twenty yards from the ship. She writhed, twisted, and rocked over onto the port side, taking on a large amount of sea water. Miraculously, the human cargo was still on deck when the wild motion ceased. Some had grabbed something solid like the rim of the hold, and others had grabbed those who had a stable hand hold. Once again, the ship had held together and they had been saved because of the depth of sea cushioning the hull from the violent explosion.

Ben looked through the window and watched the bombs raining down on the harbour. Then, with satisfaction, he noticed that Bert and Pearson had taken the initiative to start working on the manual bilge pump, in front of the wheelhouse, to drain the hold. He reached over and pulled the telegraph lever back to "Half". Looking at the officer, he said, "Ten minutes on this course and then we head out to sea."

"Indeed. It will be dark in five hours, by then we should be well up the coast of Belgium and hopefully out of this hell hole. I'll plot the course for you."

So saying, he chose a chart for the southern part of the North Sea, unfolded it and spread it on the floor.

After a short time Ben announced, "We ain't yet seen the last of it, Lieutenant."

He was on his knees, divider in hand. Looking up at Ben, he said, "How do you mean?"

"Come and look at this."

Ben had steered to avoid a large pool of black oil. Among the wreckage were sailors' hats, obviously British ones, and then a little further on, a number of sailors, face down in the black slime, supported by their life jackets.

"Oh my god! Stop the engine!"

Ben leant over and telegraphed the message. The officer grabbed his hat and went outside to the railing. He stood bolt upright and saluted the carnage in front of him. Soldiers around him who saw his gesture did the same. After a few moments, he turned and slowly walked back to the wheelhouse.

"I wonder what ship it was. What a way to end your days, poor sods."

They were both silent for a few seconds and then the lieutenant said, "Slow ahead, Captain."

He hung up his hat and then resumed his position on the floor.

Not long after, he looked up at Ben and asked, "Do you think we can make four knots on one propeller?"

"Happen we might, if the tide's good. But draggin' that hawser will slow us."

"So, perhaps I should base the course on 3 knots."

"In the circumstances, that might be wise."

Looking out of the window, Ben could see that some of the soldiers still had their field rations and water bottles with them. Many were sharing with those who had nothing. This suddenly reminded him that none of the crew had eaten for a day and a half and each had only had very little water from the now empty tank.

The officer rose to his feet and announced, "Set course nor, nor, east for ten hours. That will take us about level with the Belgian port of Zeebrugge. Not that we are going to see it, especially as it is now in German hands."

"Will we be in sight of land?"

"No, well clear. After ten hours, I'll give you a new course based on Route Y to Ramsgate."

"That'll be about two in the mornin' then?

THE MISSION OF A "LITTLE SHIP"

"Yes. We need a look out on deck through the voyage. Please arrange a watch schedule with the men."

"Aye, aye, Lieutenant."

The hours seemed to pass very slowly for those awake, and most of the soldiers were, for they had to stand. In the wheelhouse, Ben and the officer took it in turns at the wheel, an hour on an hour off, so that one of them, in turns, could doze on the floor. The only relief was when Alf appeared with a bottle hidden in a sack. The contents, shared between the helmsmen and Ted, allowed them to wet their cracked lips for the first time in twenty-four hours.

The three of them were acutely aware of the dangers that could be lurking around them. Until darkness, and at first light, there was the threat that some aircraft could be operating north of Dunkirk and might spot them. There was also the chance of encountering a German warship or the dreaded high speed E Boats. In the five hours of darkness, there was another danger, that of collision with another ship, enemy or friendly. The latter because other ships would also be using the Y Route and no vessels were permitted to use navigation lights.

In the engine room, Ted was nursing the one engine. It seemed noisier than it should have been, but was that his imagination? The effect of a heightened concern was his realisation that the lives of all on board were totally dependent on the mechanical giant under his care, tasked with getting them to a safe haven. The drag of the hawser was certainly making the engine work at its utmost to keep up speed. There was also some drag from the rudder as since the starboard propeller was driving the ship, the helmsman had to steer slightly to starboard to keep a straight course. Content that all was as well as it could be, Ted allowed himself to doze for short periods.

"Time to head for Ramsgate, Captain," said the lieutenant, waking the dozing Ben. "It's two o'clock."

Ben got up from the floor and took over the wheel. His companion once more got down on his knees and spread the chart in front of him, looking at it with his torch.

At length, he said, "If we did indeed make three knots, we are at the most northerly point on the Y Route."

"And well off the coast of Belgium."

"Exactly, your new course should be west, south, west. I am sure that later in the day we will sight other vessels coming from or going to Ramsgate. That will give us a better idea of how accurate this course is."

Turning the wheel, Ben said, "So west, sou', west it is then."

After his turn of an hour at the wheel, Ben went outside, closed the door, and lit his pipe.

"Mind if I join you, Ben?" said Alf, who had appeared through the throng of soldiers.

Ben clicked his lighter and covered the flame as best he could while Alf lit his cigarette.

"Can't you sleep, Alf?"

"Sleep don't come easy after all we've seen the last two days, do it?"

"It's goin' to take months if not years to get over this."

"We perhaps never will," answered Alf. "There's somethin' I wanted to ask you, Ben."

"What's that, mate?"

"Nipper, our fourth hand, he done a good job on this trip."

"We ain't home yet, Alf."

"True, but I got a notion that he's goin' jump ship when we gets to Ramsgate."

"Why's that, then?"

"Well, he knows that when we leave there, the next stop be Newport and that's the last place he wants to be."

"Too true. But it ain't goin' to be easy to skip ship in Ramsgate for he ain't got an identity card like we has to have."

"He'll never get out of the docks, there's bound to be loads of coppers checking folk."

"I'll put my mind to it, Alf."

"My watch soon, I'd better get back to the forecastle."

THE MISSION OF A "LITTLE SHIP"

It was just after eight in the evening when the *Bee* followed the channel markers to enter Ramsgate Harbour.

"Slow ahead, if you please, Captain. That launch is heading towards us."

"Aye, aye."

The officer put on his cap and went outside to meet the coxswain of the launch as it came alongside. Salutes were exchanged.

"Good evening, sir, how many men do you have on board?"

"Just over three hundred soldiers, four hands, the captain and me."

"Please follow me and berth on the outer mole in the harbour. The Red Cross has a reception centre."

Alf had found his way through the excited soldiers.

"How do you want it, Skipper?"

"Port side to. Get Pearson to take the stern line, Bert the bow, and you wait amidships to receive the gang plank when they push it over to us."

Soon after, they were moored and Ted heard what to him was a beautiful sound – the telegraph sounding, "Finished with Engine". Preparations were made for men to start disembarking. Along the massive concrete mole there were tables with tea urns, cups and heaps of cakes. The soldiers were shepherded towards the refreshments where they were attended to by ladies who also handed out cigarettes.

Ted emerged from the engine room and stepped over a soldier, on his knees, in prayer. Others slapped his back as he passed. Many had kind words of thanks, and one said, "Thanks, old man. I never thought that I would see my wife and kiddies again!"

Finally, the wounded were helped ashore to the Red Cross tent.

While that was happening, the lieutenant was busy collecting up his belongings and taking them to the mole. When he was ready, he called a naval rating who was one of several on duty nearby and asked for him to help carry the goods to where the officer had to report for duty.

"Ted, we got to start up again. They've asked us to move into the inner harbour to leave space here for the next ship.

With little enthusiasm, Ted mumbled, "Aye, aye, Skipper."

"And then we can all get some kip."

"The harbour master has asked you to berth alongside that collier ship, over there," said the lieutenant, pointing across to the crowded harbour. "But I will be leaving you here. I have to report for my next duty."

"What, you ain't seein' us safely back to Portsmouth, then?" asked Ted.

"I'm afraid not, Lieutenant Maynard. You will have to find your own way. You should be all right if you follow the coast."

"It would have been helpful to have had them charts you got," stated Ben.

The officer hesitated and then said, awkwardly, "I'm afraid they are Admiralty property."

There was an uncomfortable silence. It was eventually broken by the officer.

"I will arrange for some victuals to be delivered to the ship tomorrow morning, before you leave. Well, gentlemen, I can't say it has been a pleasure, but I do say that I would be honoured to serve with you men again. It might well happen; the Admiralty wants you to get repairs and then go back to Dunkirk."

Ben and Ted's eyes met, neither wanting to comment until at last Ben said, "It was an honour for us too, Sub-Lieutenant Russel. If happenstance dictates it, we'd be honoured to have you on board again.

Ben called the crew together, and in turn they shook hands with the man going ashore.

"Right, lads, we gotta raft up beside that collier, the coal ship over there. From the black dust on his deck there' no doubtin' what cargo he carries. You knows the drill, a line ashore fore and aft and same to the collier. When 'tis done, fill up the water tank and we might even get a bit of that cake."

"Aye, aye, Skipper, but you owes me a bottle of brown ale," said Alf.

"We'll take that when we gets to Newport," retorted Ben. As attractive as it sounded, he was far too tired and also, he had other plans.

Chapter 13

SUNDAY 2ND JUNE, 21.00 HOURS
RAMSGATE

It was a warm evening. Alf and Ted had both fallen asleep on a rolled-up tarpaulin on deck, and the others were well dead to the world in the crews' quarters.

When they had moored up against the other ship, Ben made a point of waving to the skipper. The man was watching through the bridge window as one of the collier's crew helped with the lines. He responded to Ben with a mime, holding his hand as if he had a beer glass in it and tipping it towards his mouth. A clear invitation which Ben wanted. The two men on the *Bee*'s deck were snoring loudly as he made his way to the bridge of the collier.

"You all right, man? Welcome to the *Mary Anne of Newcastle*. A right fine ship she is and all, if you're wantin' coal. Captain George Armstrong at your service."

"And Captain Ben Bainbridge at yours."

"Ye wouldna' be from the north, man, would ye. Bainbridge is a typical Northumberland name."

Ben was trying to adjust to the man's dialect but just managed to understand this comment.

"No, no, my folks bin born on the Isle of Wight since the time of Adam."

George laughed, stretched, and grabbed an empty glass from a rack where they sat in holes, to stop them falling down when the ship rolled.

"D'ye care for a brown ale, Ben?"

"Wouldn't say no, it wouldn't be neighbourly of me to refuse."

"This is real beer, Newcastle Broon, not like the nat's piss they drink doon sooth, man."

They lifted their glasses and knocked them together. Ben studied the man's face; he had florid cheeks and a ruby coloured nose. A nose which, judging from the crookedness of it, had at some time or perhaps times, received a blow. From the colour of his face, there was no doubt about what he used to comfort himself in the difficult moments in his very dangerous profession.

"So where is your voyage takin' yer, Captain Armstrong?"

"To Southampton. I'm stuck here waitin' for six more ships t'catch up wi' me."

"Why's that?"

"We have to sail in convoy, man, with navy escort. The Jerries try to pick us off like flies on a cheese, to stop the coal that sooth coast factories need. Most often I'm on an FS convoy."

"What'd that be?"

"We transport coal from Scotland and Newcastle to southern ports, most often London, but this one's longer. FS is "Forth to Southend". That is Firth of Forth, in Scotland. When we goes home, we are FN – "Forth to Nore in the Thames Estuary". That's for them ships as have ney bin sunk."

"Dangerous work then."

"I fancy what you've been about is much more so, man."

Ben exhaled loudly, "It was hell on earth."

"Yous goin' back?"

"No, we got to get some repairs done. Picked up a hawser in the port prop."

"Well, man, you won't get it repaired here, they're too busy with navy vessels."

"No, we's hopin' to make it back to our home port on the one engine."

"Rather you than me, man. If yous get stuck out there on the briny, no buggers goin' to help ye."

"I noticed that you only had one crew member on deck when we come in."

"Aye, man, that's my crew!" he said raising his voice. "That's all I have left, a year ago there were four hands on this ship, man."

"What happened?"

"What happened? A bloody war happened. My first mate volunteered for the navy and a deckhand decided, or rather his wife decided for him, that the coal mine was safer than voyagin' around England with a load of the stooff. I can understand the bugger, shiftin' coal under the Germans' nose is like have a target on ye back, man."

There was a silence while they both took a long draught.

"I got a spare crew member, a good lad, he's young and he wants to be a seaman, but he's got a problem."

"How young?"

"Goin' on fer seventeen."

"Jezra, the crew member you saw, would be like a father to him. He lost his son to tuberculosis three year since."

"T'would be good, the lad's an orphan."

"What's the problem you mentioned, man?"

"He ain't got an identity card."

Captain Armstrong threw his head back and roared with laughter. With his mouth wide open, Ben could not but see how few teeth he had left.

"Ben, you bin at sea for many years I would guess. There can be no more motley bunch of villains on God's earth than you finds in some crews, drunks, drug takers, bullies, sadistic creeps. You name it. A missin' identity card don't rate as a problem on a merchant ship, man."

"I'll talk to him in the mornin'. If he jumps our ship, he ain't got far to go to yours."

"When you leavin'?"

"As soon as we get a delivery of navy rations in the mornin."

"Tell him the money's good, we gets a dangerous cargo bonus. Come on, have another, man."

"No, thanks, George, it's bin a long forty-eight hours."

"Well, see you in the mornin', man."

It was dark when Ben climbed down from the bigger vessel to the *Bee*'s deck. It was very dark, but he was aware of a movement on deck.

"Who's that, come on who are ye?"

Then he tested his intuition and said in a low voice, "Pearson, hang on, I got news for ye."

There was a whisper, "'Ow did you know it was me, Skipper?"

"'Cause I knows that you be the only one on this ship whose worries might stop them from gettin' the damn good sleep they deserve."

From the sound of the voice, Ben realised that he must be standing by the mast. He made his way there.

"From what I understands, Newport don't hold any interest for 'ee."

Hesitantly, Pearson said, "Well, no, Skipper. T'aint somewhere I want to be."

"I just been talkin' to the master of the *Mary Anne*, the collier beside us. He's lookin' for crew. T'aint a pretty boat, but a good place to learn seamanship and disappear for a while so's them as is lookin' fer thee, might well tire of it."

"I ain't got an identity card."

" T'is only landlubbers as is concerned about such. It's a job where they pays good wages."

"Yeah? Will they take me?"

"With my recommendation they will. Mind you, 'tis hard, dangerous work."

"Oh, that don't matter. Can't be more risky than that we bin doin'."

"Go back to bed, you swaps ships in the mornin'."

"Thanks, Skipper."

Ben found his way to the wheelhouse. Now there was room for him to stretch out on the two sacks he kept there and sleep.

Dawn was just after four thirty, and soon after, Ramsgate Harbour came alive with activity. Some little ships were leaving for Dunkirk. Ben was woken by the *Bee* rocking violently from the wash of two hospital ships, HMHS *Paris* and SS *Maid of Orleans*, as they quickly left the harbour to continue with their work. Looking out of the window, Ben saw two minesweepers, HMS *Salamander* and HMS *Albur* chasing after the hospital ships, to escort them to the beaches.

When Ted and Alf eventually stirred, Ben gave orders.

"Ted, we leave as soon as we get the provisions the lieutenant promised us, so be prepared to get your one Bolinder goin'."

"I'd better check the fuel. How long is the voyage?"

"When we come, the officer reckoned it was about 120 sea miles. So, I reckons it will take a day and a 'alf at three knots."

"Tis the night sailin' that's goin' to be difficult," commented Alf.

"'Tis true, we'll deal with that in due course. Now, Alf, get the two lads out of bed. We got to tidy the ship up a bit. There's an 'ose on the quay. Get Bert to spray the decks off and get rid of the puke and the blood afore the sun dries it."

"What about Pearson? Is he still here, by the way, or 'as he jumped ship like we feared?"

"Pearson is goin' to leave us today, he's signin' on the collier. They're shorthanded."

Ted looked at Alf and winked.

"I thought you were up to summat, Ben! So, the lad starts earnin' a wage, then."

They all laughed and went about their tasks. A little later, a van arrived on the quay beside the *Mary Anne*. Two naval ratings, carrying cardboard boxes, climbed aboard and made their way across the collier, to the *Bee*. They handed the supplies over to willing hands.

"There's a packet for the skipper," said one of the ratings.

"That'd be me," said Ben as he stretched out his hand to take it. Written in longhand, the label said, "To Captain Ben Bainbridge".

"Tain't Christmas yet, Skipper," said Ted.

Ben ripped open the package, and something made of metal fell onto the deck.

They all looked down at the pair of dividers. Ben pulled out the other contents.

"'Tis better than Christmas, Ted."

"Sea charts!" exclaimed Alf.

"That it be! Admiralty chart C8, Dover Straits, and this other one is …. Admiralty chart C9, Beachy Head to Isle of Wight! Well, bugger, me. The lieutenant weren't so straight-laced as he seemed!"

Ben was about to discard the wrapping when he realised that there was still something heavy in the remainder of the packaging.

"And what's this, then?" he said.

"A torch, Skipper. Just what you needs for night sailin'!"

"That it be, Alf. Now we got a better chance of findin' our way."

"Glory be!" uttered Ted.

"Right, let's finish getting' the *Bee* ship shape and be off as soon as we can. Pearson, help the others and then take your stuff and I'll introduce you to your new boss."

"Thanks, Skipper, but I aint got no stuff. Just this boiler suit."

"I saw a couple of soldiers' jackets by the forecastle, take one."

Bert slapped Pearson on the back and said, "He'd better go shoppin' when he gets his wages."

Just after nine, they were ready to go, but their departure was delayed. The air raid alarm took everyone by surprise. A flag was hoisted at the harbour entrance to denote that no ship movements were permitted. Soon, the crew heard a familiar sound, the roaring of Henkel engines. The naval ships opened up with anti-aircraft fire and were effective in keeping the planes away from the harbour. The bombs all exploded at sea a safe distance away.

Captain Armstrong leant over the rail of the *Mary Anne* and shouted to Ben, "That's the first air raid Ramsgate has had, man! I'll tell 'ee what, it won't as like be the last."

Pearson appeared beside him and smiled down at his old ship mates.

As soon as the flag at the harbour entrance was lowered, the *Bee* set sail.

· · · · · · ● · · · · · · ·

It was at two in the afternoon on the fourth of June that Ben sighted the two marker buoys he was searching for, the Looe Channel. Their passage had gone without incident apart from when they passed three other ships, sister ships from Newport, all heading for Dunkirk.

High tide at Cowes was at half past four in the afternoon, and the *Bee* enjoyed a passage up the Medina as the sea flooded the channel to Newport.

As they came alongside the quay opposite the harbour master's office, an old man who had been sitting on a packing case, enjoying a pipe of tobacco, stretched his arthritic joints and hobbled over to take the *Bee*'s stern line and put the loop over a bollard.

"Where you bin? Ain't seen you fer the past week, Ben."

"You'll hear all about it soon enough," he answered.

Soon a crowd of men had gathered by the ship and questions rained on the crew. A few were answered, but very few. The crew of the *Bee* wanted to go home. Very soon, each of them, one after another, stepped onto the quay and after few wobbly steps, the effect of having been at sea for eight days on a small ship, the crew went their separate ways, haversacks over their shoulders. Ben paused a moment, turned round, and looked at the ship.

He was feeling light-headed; the lack of sleep, food, and water had taken its toll. He looked at the *Bee* and asked himself, "Did it really happen or were it a nightmare?" Then he noticed the machine gun holes and the splintered wood on the frame of the wheelhouse door. "Yes, it did happen and this little ship got us through it."

He shouldered his bag and set off for Hearne Street.

Chapter 14

12ᵀᴴ MAY, 1941 NEWPORT

Ben was just about to leave for the harbour when there was a ring of the doorbell. Molly, who was nearest, went to open the front door. There stood a man in a dark navy-blue uniform. The badge on his peaked hat stated GPO.

Molly felt a thrill, it might be a letter from Ron, her husband of just three months. She had no idea where his army posting was, and he was not allowed to tell her. But she was to be disappointed. The postman held the envelope towards her and said, "Just wanted to make sure this come to the right house. As you see, the address ain't too precise."

Molly looked at it and said, "No, it isn't is it? But this is the right place. Thanks."

The postman touched his hat with his right hand and said, "That's good, then. Bye."

Molly closed the door, turned and walked along the passageway to the living room. Ben was just doing up the strap on his haversack.

"Uncle Ben, there's a letter for you."

She handed it to him.

"You're lucky it reached you with that address – Captain Ben Bainbridge, The *Bee*, Newport, Isle of Wight."

"Who's it from then?"

"I don't know, you'll have to open it."

"I'll take it with me."

"Open it! We're intrigued to know who it's from!"

"Is it a woman's handwriting, Molly?" asked Mae.

He uttered an "um…" with the right tone to voice displeasure at her comment.

Reopening his bag, he put in the letter.

"Bye, ladies, back this evenin' usual time."

He picked up his cap and left.

The weather was mild, much milder than it was this time last year. His mind often strayed back to the most terrifying and exciting six days of his life. His exhaustion after the voyage had given way to pride in that he had been able to help save an army. The newspapers first published the story of the evacuation on the fourth of June. They claimed that three hundred and thirty-eight thousand men had been saved. Ted, who had the best head for numbers had tried to tot up how many had been taken aboard the *Bee*, but he gave up as although they had carefully counted the number they rescued on their first day, it had later become so chaotic that no one had time to consider counting. But joy about saving so many men was severely tempered by the recurring ghastly visions of the men they couldn't help and who did not even have a grave apart from an oily sea. Although they spoke little of it, he knew that the other crew members suffered the same nightmares that he did.

On his way to the harbour, he remembered that he was short of tobacco and made a detour to buy a packet. He could have a relaxing smoke while he read the letter in his pocket, when they had a break on board.

Captain George Armstrong
SS Silvia
Newcastle docks
10th May 1941

Dear Ben,
   I hope this letter reaches you for I have no other address for you. It is my assumption too that you are still alive and reached your home port safely.

THE MISSION OF A "LITTLE SHIP"

As you can see from my address, I am swinging my hammock on a different ship, also a collier.

The lad you transferred to my Mary Anne *turned out to make a fine sailor, and I thank you for pointing him in my direction. It is news about him that I write.*

On 4th March, Mary Anne *was part of a convoy of thirty-five colliers northward bound, having discharged our cargoes at Southend. HMS* Gossamer, *a minesweeper, was our escort.*

The biggest ship in the convoy was SS Corduff, *2000 tons. We were off Cromer in Norfolk, when just before midnight the convoy was attacked by E-boats. She was the first to go down, with all hands. Five others met a similar fate, including* Mary Anne. *In our case, we took a torpedo on the starboard side and the hull quickly flooded. The old girl listed badly, but it gave us time to put on life jackets.*

As the ship heeled, we climbed up the slanting deck and held on to the rail until she went right over. All three of us, though soaked with sea water, managed to climb up to the rudder, and there we sat, waiting for her to go down. The ship next to ours was on fire, so we could see what was going on. We even saw the number on the E-boat as it hove to nearby to watch. I'll never forget it, E-S28.

Men started jumping into the sea from the burning vessel, some started to swim to where we were, but they were clearly having trouble, the North Sea is very cold in March. Young Pearson could not bear to see these men struggling. He slid down the hull to sea level and struck out to help. I'm very sorry to say, that's the last we saw of him.

Mary Anne stayed afloat long enough for us to be picked up by the Cromer lifeboat. The sea is a bastard killer, but it has a lure many of us can't resist, so a month later I got command of the SS Silvia.

I don't know who Pearson was or where he came from, or even how he came to be on the Bee, but I regret having to give you this news, which I do in case he was close family of yours. He was in any case a fine lad and a brave one.

*Yours truly,
George*

EPILOGUE

Fact or fiction

As I mentioned in the introduction to this book, it is a novel, based as near as possible on fact. Readers may wonder what the balance is between fiction and fact. To this end, I recommend a read of the short but hugely informative diary written by the engineer of the *Bee*. In all my research on the subject of Operation Dynamo, this is the only contemporary, personal account by a sailor on one of the "Little Ships" that I have found. It can be seen on my website:

https://tinyurl.com/ccubzju7

The "Little Ships"

There were six ships from Newport that took part in Operation Dynamo with a total of twenty crew members, four of whom were from Portsmouth. All of them bravely volunteered to take their ships to Dunkirk. Their stories must have been similar to that of the *Bee*, but unfortunately, I have been unable to trace any written accounts of their voyages apart from their ship's logs. These give the briefest of detail but show that they arrived at Dunkirk soon after the *Bee*.

Over seven hundred craft are officially recognised as the "Little Ships of Dunkirk". They were of all types, ranging from pleasure craft to rowing lifeboats and motor barges. While the majority of soldiers rescued were embarked on the mole in the harbour, on mainly Royal Navy ships, it is estimated that a third of the men were picked up by the Little Ships. These vessels played a vital part as they were able to go inshore on the gently sloping sea bottom and embark soldiers directly from the shallow water. There they were in constant danger from the formidably effective German aircraft. Most often, these small craft transferred the saved men to larger ships offshore. The fact that most had no signalling flags or lights to communicate with the navy vessels made this task difficult. Over a hundred of the "Little Ships" were sunk, out of a total of two hundred and twenty vessels lost during the operation.

Casualties

A hundred and twenty-six personnel on the "Little Ships" were killed. The youngest, the third hand on a Thames barge, was fifteen.

The damage, destruction, and loss of ships during Operation Dynamo is on a level difficult to comprehend. The Royal Navy lost many vessels that were sunk or skuttled through necessarily putting themselves in harm's way to protect the rescuers. Six destroyers were lost in four days along with several minesweepers and many other craft. This was an awful loss but not a crippling one. In fact, according to my research, the Royal Navy had one hundred and eighty destroyers at the beginning of the war. Nevertheless, a large number of the sailors of the Royal Navy paid an awful, and in many cases an ultimate price in protecting the vessels evacuating the troops.

The hawser

At first, I was dubious about whether a ship could pick up a hawser round its propeller and then drag the heavy line over a hundred sea miles. However, in 2004, I received this unsolicited letter:

Dear Mr Wills,

My 82-year-old father saw your article in the County Press. He asked me to write to you. Dad worked as a marine fitter for Pickfords for 43 years and was working there during the Dunkirk evacuation.

He told me that when the Bee *was at Dunkirk, she picked up a hawser from a sunken ship, wrapping it around her port propeller. She returned on one engine. This action resulted in her crank shaft bearings breaking down. Dad said that he had the task of sawing the hawser off and repairing the engine. He also said that the crew on returning did not say much about what had happened to them but went straight home to families and to sleep.*

Yours faithfully
Julia F.

Colliers

Convoys of colliers were vital for supplying coal to London and other industrial centres from ports in northeast England. The ships were often old and not well-suited for tight convoy formations, making them vulnerable to enemy attacks. They faced threats from German E-boats, aircraft, mines, and even shore-based artillery. The attrition rates of these ships and the loss of merchant sailors was terrible. The German High Command had recognised that the supply of energy was all important to the south of England. Therefore, huge German resources were set upon stopping the convoys. For example, Convoy CW8, passing through the Dover Straights on 25 -26 July 1940, was attacked by around three hundred planes as well as fast torpedo boats. Nine of the twenty-one colliers were sunk.

Approved schools

These residential institutions were introduced in 1933 and existed until 1969. They were generally managed by charitable organisations. The schools were intended for juvenile offenders and for children deemed to be beyond parental control. The teaching programme was aimed very much at practical skills, such carpentry and metal work.

Approved schools were known for strict discipline, including corporal punishment. Boys could be caned on the clothed bottom and girls on the hand. Boys who absconded could be caned eight times on a clothed bottom.

The "Dad" system was explained to me by a man who was, at one time, the "Dad" in an approved school. Regrettably, for him it was the beginning of a long career in crime.

In 1968 a previous teacher at an approved school on the Isle of Wight made accusations in a national newspaper about excessive force being used at the school. He claimed that one boy had been so severely beaten by a teacher that he was deaf for two weeks, and that another boy, who was in poor physical condition, had also been beaten by a teacher and died in hospital. An investigation into the latter case found that in general, boys were only allowed to wear sports shorts when they were beaten, and it was decided that this was irregular. It was said that the headmaster, Father Cassian, was aware of this practise. The Home Secretary proposed that the headmaster's retirement should be brought forward.

The aftermath

While the massive effort of the "Little Ships" was lauded by the war government, no recognition of the superb effort of hundreds of men and women who manned the craft has ever been made, in terms of a medal, by the British Government. However, in 1960, the town of Dunkirk and a French Association of Veterans created a commemorative medal for French personnel involved. It was for

"Service in the Dunkirk Sector between the 29th of May and the 3rd of June 1940."

In 1970 this was extended to Allied forces, including civilian volunteers – the crews of the "Little Ships". Thus, the sixteen men from Newport could at last claim a medal.

OTHER BOOKS BY MICHAEL E WILLS

Izar, The Amesbury Archer This is the story of a man who lived 4,500 years ago. His skeleton is in Salisbury Museum. He was born in the region of the Swiss Alps and died nearly a thousand miles away in the south of England near to Stonehenge, when it was being built. The mystery is how this could have happened, for the man's skeleton shows that he was physically disabled.

He lived at the end of an era, when human curiosity was pushing the boundaries into a new age. It was an exciting time when dependence on stone gave way to a new, more versatile material – metal.

The numerous items buried with the man give tantalising clues as to his ability as an archer, but also to his role as a pioneer metal worker.

"Izar's life has been moulded around what little is known about him, and the result is a novel full of intense detail with a gripping narrative." The Coffee Pot Book Club"

http://tiny.cc/9nrt001

Finn's Fate tells the story of three brothers in tenth century Scandinavia. Their home is north of the Arctic Circle in an isolated region populated by the Sami, the Laplanders. The living is harsh and the climate unforgiving. After a disastrous fire at their homestead, they decide to ignore their family's wishes and abandon their home. The young men embark on a journey to find a better life. They undertake a lengthy odyssey through unfriendly territory and dangerous seas. Through storms and battles they support each other and become increasingly wealthy as they raid the unprotected villages and ports on the British coast. Their success leads them to a dangerous level of confidence and they embark on one raid too many. The book mirrors actual historical events and offers a solution to a real mystery in the Dorset countryside.

"*It's an extremely gripping book that entices the reader to keep going onto the next chapter despite the clock now reading 2am.*" – The Historical Novel Society

http://tiny.cc/dnrt001

Three Kings – One Throne The eleventh century was the most turbulent time in English history with six kings in sixty years. "Three Kings, One Throne" charts the lives of characters real and imaginary who get caught up in the maelstrom of treachery, carnage, greed, lust and loyalty. In part the novel describes the true story of how the most successful and experienced soldier of the eleventh century, once a member of the elite bodyguard of the Turkish Emperor, launched the biggest ever invasion of England with sixteen thousand men in three hundred ships. An invasion which dwarfed that of Duke William of Normandy in October 1066.

The crown of England was the most contested in Europe, this is the story of three men; two kings and one duke, soon to be a king, and the men and women who fought and died for their causes.

"*Michael Wills has done an admirable job in bringing together all the intricate historical details and has woven a credible tale of adventure and political skulduggery.*" – Jaffa Reads Too

http://tiny.cc/fnrt001

The Wessex Turncoat Aaron Mew is a seventeen year-old apprentice blacksmith living in a small English village, in the late eighteenth century. His life is simple yet secure, until the day when he volunteers to take the place of his father on an errand for the squire.

The country boy is wrenched from the environment in which he grew up and thrust into a world of ruffians, drunks, criminals and disgraced professionals – part of the army of George III. An army desperately short of men, but with the huge ambition to quell the rebellion in America and to retain the country under British rule.

After relentless training, Aaron's regiment, the 62nd Regiment of Foot, is posted to Canada. There, fighting side by side with First Nation braves and German allies, the boy soldier becomes a hardened warrior.

The *Wessex Turncoat* tells the story of an ambitious military campaign and the fate of a regiment which was sacrificed mainly because of the vanity and intransigence of an English general.

"*I can't stress enough the how I loved the expertise and the countless research hours put into each and every page, as well as the quality of the dialogue of ordinary soldiers.*" Alaric Longward, The Review, USA

http://tiny.cc/knrt001

One Decent Thing Aberystwyth in 1971, Scottie, a self-centered, decadent university administrator with a weakness for cigarettes, drink and women, finds that he is unwelcome when he visits his university student daughter, Tina. His effort to drown his sorrows leads him into a world of terrorism and danger where he becomes a fugitive from the police and from the IRA. In desperation and with the help of some university students, he decides to break with his egocentric habits and do one decent thing. But he has made powerful enemies and will have to face retribution.

"*A very enjoyable and exciting book. As the book goes on, it gets increasingly more tense and I found myself reading quickly to see what happens next! The action is well-paced and left me on the edge of my seat*"

http://tiny.cc/nnrt001

For the Want of Silver For three decades, Ulf of Borresta carved a path of blood and silver across England. He was no mere warrior—he was a Viking raider who amassed a staggering fortune in Danegeld, the extortion money paid by desperate English monarchs to keep the Norsemen at bay. In the churchyard of Orkesta, Sweden, two ancient rune stones bear witness to Ulf's legacy. They speak of a man who stood alongside the most feared Viking chieftains—real figures etched into history—plundering towns, burning villages, and battling for wealth and power. The battles which Ulf profited from are all named in the Anglo-Saxon Chronicles.

But Ulf's story is more than a chronicle of conquest. It is a visceral tale of ambition, survival, and the brutal world of the Viking Age. From the storm-wracked shores of Scandinavia to the blood-soaked fields of England, this novel brings to life the reign of terror that shaped a continent—and the man who profited from it.

Inspired by true events, this gripping historical epic plunges you into the heart of the Viking world, where the price of power was measured in silver and blood.

"I'm happy to recommend this novel to anybody who enjoys well-plotted historical novels with strong characterisation."

A 'Wishing Shelf' Book Review www.thewsa.co.uk
http://tiny.cc/vnrt001

Michael E Wills was born on the Isle of Wight, UK, and educated at Carisbrooke Grammar and St Peter's College, Birmingham. After a long career in education, as a teacher, a teacher trainer and textbook writer, in retirement he took up writing historical novels. His first book, *Finn's Fate*, was followed by a sequel novel, *Three Kings – One Throne*. In 2015, he started on a  quartet of Viking stories for young readers called, Children of the Chieftain. The first book, *Betrayed*, was described by the Historical Novel Society reviewer as "An absolutely excellent novel which I could not put down" and long-listed for the Historical Novel Society 2016 Indie Prize. The second book in the quartet, *Banished*, was published in December 2015 followed in 2017 by the third book, *Bounty*. *Bound For Home* completed the series in 2019. His book for younger children, Sven and the Purse of Silver, won bronze medal in the Wishing Shelf Book Awards. His most recent books are from periods in history with an enormous time span between them. *Izar, The Amesbury Archer*, (runner-up for Coffee Pot Book Club indie historical fiction book of the year 2021) is based in the Neolithic period. a Viking story, *For the Want of Silver*, is based on the message carved on an actual runestone and an award winning series of children's books called *The Children of Clifftop Farm*, is about WW2.

Though a lot of his spare time is spent with grandchildren, he also has a wide range of interests including researching for future books, writing, playing the guitar, carpentry and electronics.

You can find out more about Michael E Wills and the books he has written by visiting his website: www.michaelwills.eu

www.ingramcontent.com/pod-product-compliance
Lightning Source LLC
Chambersburg PA
CBHW072018070526
44583CB00015B/1530